DON
DeLILLO

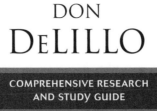

EDITED AND WITH AN
INTRODUCTION BY HAROLD BLOOM

CURRENTLY AVAILABLE

DON
DeLILLO

COMPREHENSIVE RESEARCH
AND STUDY GUIDE

BLOOM'S

MAJOR
NOVELISTS

EDITED AND WITH AN INTRODUCTION
BY HAROLD BLOOM

CHELSEA HOUSE
PUBLISHERS
A Haights Cross Communications Company
Philadelphia

First Printing
1 3 5 7 9 8 6 4 2

Library of Congress Cataloging-in-Publication Data
Don DeLillo / edited and with an introduction by Harold Bloom.
        p. cm. —(Bloom's major novelists)
Includes bibliographical references and index.
    ISBN 0-7910-7031-X
    1. DeLillo, Don—Criticism and interpretation. I. Bloom, Harold. II.
Series.
    PS3554.E4425 Z643 2002
    813'.54—dc21

                                                            2002151395

Chelsea House Publishers
1974 Sproul Road, Suite 400
Broomall, PA 19008-0914

http://www.chelseahouse.com

Contributing Editor: Anne Marie Albertazzi

Cover design by Terry Mallon

Layout by EJB Publishing Services

CONTENTS

USER'S GUIDE

This volume is designed to present biographical, critical, and bibliographical information on the author and the author's best-known or most important novels. Following Harold Bloom's editor's note and introduction is a concise biography of the author that discusses major life events and important literary accomplishments. A critical analysis of each novel follows, tracing significant themes, patterns, and motifs in the work. An annotated list of characters supplies brief information on the main characters in each novel.

A selection of critical extracts, derived from previously published material, follows each thematic analysis. In most cases, these extracts represent the best analysis available from a number of leading critics. Because these extracts are derived from previously published material, they will include the original notations and references when available. Each extract is cited, and readers are encouraged to use the original publications as they continue their research. A bibliography of the author's writings, a list of additional books and articles on the author and their work, and an index of themes and ideas conclude the volume.

As with any study guide, this volume is designed as a supplement to the works being discussed, and is in no way intended as a replacement for those works. The reader is advised to read the text prior to using this study guide, and to keep it accessible for quick reference.

ABOUT THE EDITOR

Harold Bloom is Sterling Professor of the Humanities at Yale University and Henry W. and Albert A. Berg Professor of English at the New York University Graduate School. He is the author of over 20 books, and the editor of more than 30 anthologies of literary criticism.

Professor Bloom's works include *Shelley's Mythmaking* (1959), *The Visionary Company* (1961), *Blake's Apocalypse* (1963), *Yeats* (1970), *A Map of Misreading* (1975), *Kabbalah and Criticism* (1975), *Agon: Toward a Theory of Revisionism* (1982), *The American Religion* (1992), *The Western Canon* (1994), and *Omens of Millennium: The Gnosis of Angels, Dreams, and Resurrection* (1996). *The Anxiety of Influence* (1973) sets forth Professor Bloom's provocative theory of the literary relationships between the great writers and their predecessors. His most recent books include *Shakespeare: The Invention of the Human*, a 1998 National Book Award finalist, *How to Read and Why* (2000), and *Genius: A Mosaic of One Hundred Exemplary Creative Minds* (2002).

Professor Bloom earned his Ph.D. from Yale University in 1955 and has served on the Yale faculty since then. He is a 1985 MacArthur Foundation Award recipient and served as the Charles Eliot Norton Professor of Poetry at Harvard University in 1987–88. In 1999 he was awarded the prestigious American Academy of Arts and Letters Gold Medal for Criticism. Professor Bloom is the editor of several other Chelsea House series in literary criticism, including BLOOM'S MAJOR SHORT STORY WRITERS, BLOOM'S MAJOR NOVELISTS, BLOOM'S MAJOR DRAMATISTS, BLOOM'S MODERN CRITICAL INTERPRETATIONS, BLOOM'S MODERN CRITICAL VIEWS, and BLOOM'S BIOCRITIQUES.

EDITOR'S NOTE

This volume offers critical insights into what are taken to be Don DeLillo's five principal novels to date: *The Names, Mao II, Libra, White Noise,* and the monumental *Underworld.*

My Introduction centers upon the terroristic bewilderments of *Mao II.*

On *The Names,* I particularly commend John A. McClure's illuminating study of the novel's final fragment.

Mao II is usefully juxtaposed with the art of Andy Warhol by Jeffrey Karnicky.

The commentary by Frank Lentricchia on *Libra* has assumed a kind of classic status.

White Noise, which invites commentary, is so well served by all the Critical Views here that I shall not choose between them.

Underworld, a novel still not fully comprehended, has a suggestive note by David Remnick on the effect of a passage by John Cheever upon DeLillo's vision. Tony Tanner's critique of *Underworld* remains the best informed challenge to the book.

Harold Bloom

In different ways, I prefer *White Noise*, *Libra*, and *Underworld* to *Mao II*, but a crucial element of Don DeLillo's achievement is his uncanny, proleptic sense of the triumph of the Age of Terror, which is the peculiar strength of *Mao II*. In 2002, *Mao II* is the way we live now, in the Age of George W. Bush, John Ashcroft, and Osama bin Laden. One can venture that character is irrelevant to DeLillo because he has a good claim to have invented those clearly fictive personages: Dubya, Ashcroft, Osama. As for plot, what relevance can it have in a cosmos where *everything* can turn out to be part of a terror scheme. That may seem the anarcho-sadism of Thomas Pynchon, whose earlier, paranoid visions were the prime precursors of DeLillo. And yet Pynchonian paranoia was systematic; DeLillon paranoia retains a random element, which probably has something to do with the Romantic Transcendentalism that somehow lingers in DeLillo.

DeLillo is soft-spoken, without pretense, a man of good will. You could not insert him into one of his novels, not even as Nick Shay in *Underworld*. He is the antitype of *Mao II*'s Bill Gray, despite some superficial resemblances. Gray, like Pynchon, hides himself in order to write, but dies as a witness to a new reality, in which the terrorist has usurped the novelist. East Beirut, where the novel closes, is the New Everywhere.

A novel that begins in Yankee Stadium (sacred ground for DeLillo and myself), with 6,500 couples simultaneously being married by the Reverend Moon ends with an East Beirut wedding escorted by a tank and jeep mounted with a recoilless rifle. And all this would be routine, were it not for the intimations of a pathos, almost a transcendence, that DeLillo imparts to that final vision of marriage:

> Civilians talking and laughing and well dressed, twenty adults and half as many children, mostly girls in pretty dresses and white knee-stockings and patent-leather shoes. And here is the stunning thing that takes her a moment to understand, that this is a wedding party going by. The bride and groom carry

champagne glasses and some of the girls hold sparklers that send off showers of excited light. A guest in a pastel tuxedo smokes a long cigar and does a dance around a shell hole, delighting the kids. The bride's gown is beautiful, with lacy appliqué at the bodice, and she looks surprisingly alive, they all look transcendent, free of limits and unsurprised to be here. They make it seem only natural that a wedding might advance in resplendence with a free-lance tank as escort. Sparklers going. Other children holding roses tissued in fern. Brita is gripping the rail. She wants to dance or laugh or jump off the balcony. It seems completely possible that she will land softly among them and walk along in her pajama shirt and panties all the way to heaven.

If there is a DeLillon counter-force to the Age of Terror, it must be there: "they all look transcendent, free of limits." We learn to recognize a DeLillo scene from such near-epiphanies. Unlike most of his critics, DeLillo has an Emersonian longing for the transcendental and extraordinary, for privileged moments.

How permanent an achievement is *Mao II*, compared to *Underworld?* Let it be affirmed at once that DeLillo does *not* write Period Pieces, as Updike and Bellow go on doing. Bill Gray is a sad creation, and yet his aesthetic dignity is considerable. He is an authentic writer deeply fearful that the new Time of Terror renders his art irrelevant. Samuel Beckett could alter consciousness; Bill Gray knows that he cannot. Any bomb-thrower is far more competent to modify our consciousness of reality.

It is disconcerting to reread *Mao II* just eleven years after its publication, and one year after the destruction of the World Trade Center. What shocked us must have confirmed DeLillo in his anguished apprehension of reality. *Mao II* in time may seem like secondary DeLillo, but it will lose its wisdom only if someday we pass out of our unhappy time.

BIOGRAPHY OF

Don DeLillo

The son of Italian immigrants, Don DeLillo was born on November 20, 1936 and grew up in the Italian-American Fordham section of the Bronx in New York City. He was raised and educated as a Catholic and attended Cardinal Hayes High School, then Fordham University, where he graduated in 1958 with a degree in communication arts. DeLillo recalls being asleep or unaffected through high school or college, but stated in a 1982 interview with the *New York Times Book Review* that "New York itself was an enormous influence" and that he found inspiration in "the paintings in the Museum of Modern Art, the music at the Jazz Gallery and the Village Vanguard, the movies of Fellini and Godard and Howard Hawks."

In 1959 DeLillo moved to Manhattan and, unable to break into the publishing business, began work as a copywriter for Ogilvy & Mather advertising agency while writing fiction on the side. His first short story, "The River Jordan," was published in *Epoch* magazine in 1960, followed by several other stories in *Epoch*, *The Kenyon Review*, and *Carolina Quarterly*. In 1971, seven years after he quit his advertising job in favor of freelance writing, DeLillo published his first novel, *Americana* about a television executive who goes to the desert and assesses his life. His next novel, *End Zone*, about a career college football player who ends up on a deteriorating football team, was published in 1972, followed by a novel about a rock star entitled *Great Jones Street* in 1973.

DeLillo married Barbara Bennett, a landscape designer, in 1975. In 1976, his novel *Ratner's Star* was published, followed by *Players* in 1977 and *Running Dog* in 1978. *Ratner's Star*, about a mathematical genius, was the product of three years' work, including extensive research in mathematics. DeLillo recalls in a 1993 interview in the *Paris Review*: "I was drawn to the beauty of scientific language, the mystery of numbers, the idea of pure mathematics as a secret history and secret language." The theme of language and its mysterious ordering power became a theme in much of his work. *The Engineer of Moonlight*, a two-act play, was published in 1979. During the same year, DeLillo received a Guggenheim Fellowship and was thus able to travel to Greece, where he began work on *The Names*, which was published in 1982. Most critics considered *The Names* to signal a new direction away from the fantasy of his earlier novels toward a new realism. For the first time, DeLillo's work was receiving prominent critical attention.

DeLillo's next work, an essay on the Kennedy assassination entitled "American Blood: A Journey through the Labyrinth of Dallas and JFK," was published in *Rolling Stone* in 1983, followed by "Human Moments in World War III," published in *Esquire* that same year. He received an Award in Literature from the American Academy of Arts and Letters in 1984. The following year, *White Noise* was published, and it received a National Book Award. *White Noise* has been considered DeLillo's breakthrough novel, as it attracted a wider audience and gained him literary stardom.

Shortly after he finished *White Noise*, DeLillo began working on his next novel, *Libra*, an expression of the enormous influence the JFK assassination had on him and on the relationship between mass media and American mythmaking. Meanwhile, his play *The Day Room* was performed at the American Repertory Theater in Cambridge, Massachusetts and the Manhattan Theater Club in New York City in 1987. In 1988 *Libra* was published; it won the Irish Times-Aer Lingus International Fiction Prize, reached the *New York Times* bestseller list, and was nominated for the National Book Award. A fictionalized account of the life of Lee Harvey Oswald and the labyrinthine intelligence surrounding the assassination of John F. Kennedy, *Libra* was a reflection of DeLillo's sense that the assassination was the defining moment not only in his own life but in American culture thus far.

The same year, DeLillo published several short pieces, including an essay on Nazism entitled "Silhouette City: Hitler, Manson and the Millennium," which appeared in *Dimensions*, the journal of the Anti-Defamation League of B'nai B'rith. In 1991, DeLillo began work on his next novel, *Mao II*, about a reclusive author. This novel was in part a response to the Ayatollah

Khomeini's condemnation of Salman Rushdie to death for writing against Islam in *The Satanic Verses* (1989). While DeLillo continued to work on *Mao II*, his play *The Rapture of the Athlete Assumed* (1990) was performed by the American Repertory Theater. In 1991, *Mao II* was published, and in 1992, it won the PEN/Faulkner Award for Fiction. Two years later, DeLillo co-wrote a pamphlet with novelist Paul Auster in support of Salman Rushdie, and a stage adaptation of *Libra*, directed by actor John Malkovich, was performed at the Steppenwolf theater in Chicago.

In 1997, DeLillo's essays "The Artist Naked in a Cage" and "The Power of History" were published in the *New Yorker* and the *New York Times Magazine*, respectively. In the same year, his next novel, *Underworld*, was published. A bestseller in many countries including the United States, this contemplation of toxic refuse through fictional characters who survive the Cold War was lauded by critics and received a nomination for the National Book Award. In 1999 it received the Jerusalem Prize, and in 2000, the William Dean Howells Medal of the American Academy and Institute of Arts and Letters.

DeLillo's most recent play, *Valparaiso*, about a man whose travel mishap makes him the obsessive focus of the media, premiered at the American Repertory Theatre in 1999. DeLillo's latest novel, *The Body Artist* (2001), concerns a young widow who discovers and communicates with an intruder in her summer home. DeLillo has also published one book under the pseudonym Cleo Birdwell, entitled *Amazons* (1980), which is about the first woman ever to play in the National Hockey League. A member of the Academy of Arts and Letters, DeLillo lives with his wife in a suburb of New York City.

The Names

The first section of *The Names* is entitled "The Island" and refers to Kouros, an obscure island in the Cycladic group in Greece. James Axton, the 38 year-old narrator, is an American expatriate whose business keeps him traveling; his wife Kathryn and son Tap live on Kouros. Kathryn, now separated from James after eleven years, is assisting on an archaeological excavation of Minoan artifacts on the south end of the island, and Tap, aged 9, is writing a novel.

James lives in a residential area on the slopes of Lycabettus Hill in Athens, and visits Kathryn and Tap often in Kouros, where they are usually joined by a family friend named Owen Brademas, an archaeologist who heads the excavation that Kathryn assists. After this particular visit to Kouros, James returns to Athens and meets with his boss, a man named George Rowser who sells terrorist insurance to multinational executives. James is a risk analyst for Rowser; he organizes and reproduces information that flows into Athens from control points around the Mediterranean, Gulf, and Arabian Sea. James' ability to order information, and the solace he gets from it, is a recurring theme as the novel progresses.

That evening, James has dinner with a group of friends, American corporate transients like himself—all well-versed in the airports of the world. They include David Keller, a banker, and his second wife Lindsay; Richard (Dick) and Dorothy (Dot) Borden; Andreas Eliades, a Greek businessman who mistakes James for David Keller; Charles Maitland, a security consultant for the overseas branches of British and American corporations, and his wife Ann; and a German man named Stahl who is supposedly in the refrigerator business with Andreas Eliades. Later that night, James and David talk on David's terrace, where James reveals that his marriage began to deteriorate when Kathryn found out he slept with a friend of hers and she charged at him with a potato peeler. David says he knew his first marriage was over when he and his wife began watching television in separate rooms. David tells James his bank gives sizable loans to Turkey and secretly reroutes the paperwork through Athens.

The news comes out that the body of an old man was found bludgeoned to death in an isolated village called Mikro Kamini. James visits Kathryn and Tap in Kouros; Owen arrives having just visited the village to gather information from the locals. Later Owen tells James he has been surprised to find out that Tap's novel, a prairie saga, is based on the stories he told the boy of his own childhood as a plowboy. Since Owen's excavation will be completed soon, Kathryn and James agree that she will take Tap to London next summer and stay with her sister.

Tap visits James in Athens for two days with his friend Rajiv and Rajiv's father Anand Dass, who works with Owen at the excavation site. Anand tells James of another case of bludgeoning a year prior on the island of Donoussa, where a young crippled girl was killed with a hammer. James visits Charles Maitland, who tells him that Iranian Oil Services Personnel are taking refuge in Athens. While Charles naps, Ann tells James that she and Charles are having marital problems due to an affair she had.

On James' next visit to Kouros, Kathryn tells James she had a visit from their old friend Frank Volterra, a filmmaker they were close to when they lived in California. Frank has come in search of information from Owen about the cult responsible for the bludgeoning murders. This news reignites James' jealousy over the sexual tension between Kathryn and Frank that has always existed. Owen arrives at the house, bringing news of another murder: an old woman in a village at the edge of the Wadi Rum, the sandstone desert in the southern part of the country, was killed with a hammer.

James finds out from Anand that the archaeological dig will be taken over by the University of Pennsylvania. James realizes that this means that Kathryn will not go to London and is angry with her for keeping this information from him. They argue bitterly. When Kathryn takes a job with the British Columbia Provincial museum, James senses the marriage is over.

The second part of the novel is entitled "The Mountain" and is set in the winter that the American hostages were taken in Iran. On his business travels in Amman, Jordan, James meets Frank

Volterra, who is on his way to Jerusalem, as advised by Owen, to obtain secret information about the cult. James travels with Frank and his lover Del Nearing to Jerusalem, where they meet a man named Vosdanik, who tells them the cult was last seen north of Damascus. Curiously, the cult speaks Aramic, which happens to be the language of Jesus, and the members engraved the initials of their victim on the murder weapon.

Back in Athens, Owen visits James in his office, where James tells him he has solved the mystery of the cult murders: they kill people whose initials match the initials of the place in which they reside. Over the holiday season, James and Tap drive through the Mani, mountains southwest of Argos. As they drive, they come across a fallen boulder on which the words "Ta Onomata" are painted in white, meaning "The Names." James thinks this is the work of the cult. For James, this new insight is a not only an intellectual breakthrough; it gives him a new sense of purpose: the cult's ritualism and linguistic purity offer him solace amidst the chaotic spin of his own life. As James' life experiences become more random and jolting, his insight on the cult mystery becomes more ordered and clear. The persistence of the ordering instinct amidst the randomness of experience highlights an aspect of DeLillo's own novel writing and of language itself.

James goes to the village where the cult supposedly resides and sees Frank there. Frank wants to make a film about the cult and is trying to get one of their members, Andahl, to persuade the others to agree to be filmed. James meets Andahl, who confirms James' theory about the initials. In Athens, Ann Maitland calls James to tell him she is worried that Andreas Eliades, her lover, is spying on him. He has been probing her for information on James.

In the third section, "The Desert," James finds out from Hardeman, a friend of David Keller, that Andreas has resigned from his firm rather than be moved to London. James is now afraid that Andreas is staying in Athens to trail him. Rowser summons James to Lahore, Pakistan, where in front of a Moghul tomb he tells James he is thinking of resigning from their company, the Northeast Group. Forebodingly, he advises James to resign as well. On the tomb is etched the 99 names of God.

The next morning, James visits Owen at Punjab University and hears of Owen's recent travels to Rajsamand and Hawa Mandir. As Owen tells his story, he becomes the narrator and we shift to his consciousness in the moment of his experiences. In Rajsamand, Owen visits a marble stepped embankment on which is inscribed an epic poem of 1017 lines in classical Sanskrit. In Hawa Mandir, Owen finds the last surviving cell of the cult, including two unnamed men, two men named Avtar Singh and Emmerich, and a woman named Bern. Owen hides out in the cult's silo while they kill their last victim, a man named Hamir Mazmudar. After the murder, he leaves with Singh and Emmerich. Then Owen narrates a flashback of his childhood in which a fanatical preacher urges him to "Let the spirit knock you free" (306). Owen concludes that the cult had no deep meaning or intention other than to match the initials of the name to the place-name.

When James returns to Athens, Charles tells him he found out the Northeast Group is a cover for the CIA. James now realizes why Rowser wanted him to resign, and immediately does so. While James is out jogging near his residence, he hears three shots fired, sees a gunman escape, and finds David Keller shot, speaking of two gunmen who pursued him. While David is in the hospital, James wonders if he was the intended victim and if Andreas was behind the shooting—Andreas did confuse him with David Keller once before.

The final section, an excerpt from Tap's novel, is called "The Prairie." Written with misspellings so glaring that the words seem oddly textured and sculptured, the story concerns a boy on the prairie named Orville Benton. In a Pentecostal church, Orville watches in wonder and terror as members of the congregation speak in tongues. When pressured by the preacher to speak in tongues as well, he tries unsuccessfully, then is overwhelmed and runs out of the church into a thunderstorm.

The Names

James Axton is the narrator. He is based in Athens and travels throughout Greece and the Middle East as a risk analyst for a firm that, unbeknownst to him, is a cover for the CIA. Separated from his wife Kathryn, James feels his life is beginning to lose meaning, but he finds meaning again in investigating and discovering the secrets of a murderous cult who bludgeons its victims to death.

Kathryn Axton is James' wife, though they are separated. She works as an assistant and report writer for Owen Brademas who is running an excavation on the Greek island of Kouros. Though she has switched jobs often in the past, she has found, in the absence of a satisfying marriage, new meaning in digging for artifacts. After Owen's dig has ended, she takes a job with the British Columbia Provincial Museum, taking their son Tap with her.

Tap, or **Thomas Arthur Axton**, gets his nickname from his dead grandfather, Thomas Arthur Pattison. He is nine years old and the son of James and Kathryn. A precocious child, he is working on a novel that is based on the early life of Owen Brademas when he was a plowboy on the prairie.

Owen Brademas is an archaeologist and a close friend of the Axton family. He runs an excavation of the Minoan civilization on the island of Kouros. An avid researcher of inscriptions, or epigraphy, he follows and investigates the murderous cult, determining that the only significance their acts bear is matching their victims' initials to the names of the villages in which they are killed.

Charles Maitland is a security consultant. Based in Athens to overseas branches of British and American corporations, he is friends with James and Kathryn. Charles' marriage goes awry when his wife has an affair, and eventually he is transferred to London. Before he goes, he informs James that James' parent company is affiliated with the CIA.

Ann Maitland is Charles' wife and the lover of Andreas Eliades. In the course of her affair with Andreas, he asks her often for information about James. This worries her so she tells James that Andreas might be a spy for an anti-CIA group.

George Rowser is James' boss. He has three verifiable identities. Though his company is affiliated with the CIA, he does not reveal this to James. When he resigns, he advises James to do the same, alluding vaguely to the affiliation, but James does not understand. James finds out later about the CIA connection and it leads him to believe that Andreas knew and wanted him killed.

David Keller is a friend of James and a banker with Mainland Bank in Athens, which secretly uses this branch to approve sizeable loans to Turkey. David Keller is shot while jogging, and James believes that Andreas is behind it. James thinks that the bullets were meant for him, since Andreas confused him with Keller once before.

Andreas Eliades is a Greek who socializes with the group of Americans in Athens who are James' friends. He is in the refrigerator business in Bremen, but he resigns when he finds out that his firm would move him to London. This act, in addition to his affair with Ann Maitland, in which he asks her incessant questions about James, leads both Ann and James to suspect that he is a spy for an anti-American group.

Anand Dass works with Owen on the excavation and is the father of Tap's friend, Rajiv. He informs James about the murder of a crippled girl on the island of Donoussa.

Frank Volterra is a successful filmmaker who was a close friend of James' and Katherine's when they were all struggling in Palo Alto, California. After many years, he reenters their life when he pays a visit to Kathryn and Owen looking for information on the cult murders, which he plans to film. James is still jealous of the affections that his wife has for Frank, and withholds key information about the cult from Frank as revenge.

Avtar Singh is one of the last surviving cult members. He and his fellow members Emmerich, Bern, and two unnamed men are hiding out in a silo when Owen arrives to observe them. Singh announces to Owen that he is member of their cult when Owen guesses that they are waiting for their victim to enter town.

CRITICAL VIEWS ON

The Names

DAVID BOSWORTH ON STASIS

[David Bosworth is the author of *The Death of Descartes*
(1981), a collection of short fiction. In this excerpt,
Bosworth calls the novel's stasis both an accomplishment
and a downfall.]

Our means to contend with death, according to DeLillo, is, of
course, language. Words are our defense against the one
explanation for events we can never accept: randomness. The
awful sacrilege of the cult is to use the very instrument of our
protection—our names, our naming—as a weapon against us,
just as, on a grander scale, the Nazis used all the instruments of
higher civilization—medicine, technology, the intricacies of
rational social planning—to perform the most monstrously
uncivilized of acts, the maintenance of a bureaucracy of death.
This profound if simple observation about the nature of
terrorism is just one feature in DeLillo's complex metaphorical
examination of contemporary life. Indeed, Axton himself can be
seen as emblematic of the author's grim view of modern man: a
stranger abroad, lost in a sea of incomprehensible signs, without
beliefs, without metaphysical answers, forced by their absence to
improvise his own theories, to surround the "bare act" of
existence with his own "desperate speculations," aware though
that these theories are "mainly for his own comfort," illusions to
succor, aware that in the end he'll be "left with nothing"—
"nothing signified, nothing meant."
    Whether we accept this view as fundamentally true, as
DeLillo appears to, or merely as an illusion characteristic of the
times, it is nevertheless an accurate expression of this century's
central spiritual dilemma. And there is much else to admire in
this truly contemporary novel beyond the clarity and significance
of its theme: a verbal vivacity, an almost effortless flow of witty
conversation, an ease in depicting a variety of settings.
    But it must be said, too, that *The Names* is a curiously static

book. One would never guess that a novel about cult murders and CIA plots, written by a man of DeLillo's obvious gifts, could be a slow read, and yet *The Names* never quite acquires the pace or urgency its subject matter would seem to guarantee. Only the tension between Axton and his wife is rendered dramatically with emotional as well as intellectual resonance—and then, too abruptly it seems, Kathryn leaves. The cult, which is more a cerebral puzzle than a physical threat, more reported to Axton than experienced by him, and the CIA-terrorist subplot, which is evolved too late and indifferently paced, are strangely unexciting. They seem too frail a narrative skeleton, thin-wired hangers, upon which to drape the heavy flesh of DeLillo's theme. The author's talents, I think, undo him here. A lesser writer could not hold our attention, as DeLillo does with his sentence by sentence virtuosity, without more carefully attending to the theatrical rhythms of the novel's plot. But in *The Names* we read on anyway, tempted by the author's well-turned phrases, unusually lucid observations, gradually aware, though, that this performance, for all its flair, is somehow less than satisfying.

DeLillo himself senses the problem. At least three times, he has Axton, in his first-person narration, observe self-consciously that the reader will want less "reflection," more fast-paced scenes and dramatic action. But to prediagnose the complaints of one's readers is not to cure them. And to pretend so is, ironically, to mimic the error of the book's own cult members, their fixation on the totemic power of language, the author relying on magic instead of performance, hoping that through the mere act of "naming" his fiction's faults, he can, like demons, cast them out.

It is possible, I suppose, that the book's slow pace is a conscious strategy: that matching style to theme, DeLillo is striving to carve a kind of fictional glyph: a stately, static, abstract pattern, one of those "letter shapes" which so fascinate Owen. But fiction, unlike graphics, is a narrative art: it exists in time. Its pattern is not simultaneous but extended and rhythmic—it is by its nature inescapably dramatic. This does not mean that gunfire and ripped bodices are necessary; even the subtlest intellectual analyses can be dramatically rendered, as Henry James was fond of demonstrating. It does mean, however, that the subject matter, whatever its nature, must evolve over time. Ideas, if they are central to a novel's existence, must come into being; they must develop for the characters and for the reader with a growing sense of discovery, carry the force of a revelation. The ideas and analyses in *The Names*, despite the wit and cogency of their exposition, are less compelling because they are not successfully dramatized, because they are not developed so much and described ... and described ... and described again.

I stress this specific lapse because it relates to the one consistent weakness to be found in DeLillo's otherwise impressive work: the power of his individual prose moments too rarely seems to gain momentum; the cumulative effect of his book-length fiction always seems less than the prospective sum of its dazzling segments. Plots don't resolve, they spin out into space. Books don't surge so much as fade away. There is a certain honest logic to this situation; the occasional shapelessness of DeLillo's novels does, in a sense, reflect their subject matter—the age's air of spiritual chaos. No one would argue that our best writers should not be documenting this loss of faith, of vision, this fear we share that our lives are not ruled by any larger rhythms. But DeLillo in his sincere depiction of the modern condition, seems too often to become its victim. His fiction, like his characters, is too often trapped in a kind of atomistic, moment-to-moment existence that strains even his considerable talent for improvisation.

To capture somehow the confusion and despair of contemporary life without in the process submitting to them, without committing the esthetic sin of the "imitative fallacy," is one of the most urgent challenges confronting fiction today. Because Don DeLillo dares to track the deepest sources of our discontent rather than merely to record its mannerisms, he has always seemed to be uniquely qualified to meet this challenge. If he hasn't yet, his failure arises from the difficulty of the task and not, as with so much fiction of the day, from an inexcusable lack of effort. Here is a man whose books should be read. A novelist of high purpose, of rare ambition, whose ongoing examination of our present-tense lives amuses and astounds us even as it educates. To say we expect more from him is an implicit if impatient compliment—a measure of this writer's special gifts.

—David Bosworth, "The Fiction of Don DeLillo." *Boston Review* 8, no. 2 (April 1983): p. 30.

Paula Bryant on Language Obsession in the Novel

[Paula Bryant's essays have appeared in *Extrapolation: A Journal of Science Fiction and Fantasy* and *Bulletin of Bibliography*. In this excerpt, Bryant traces the progression of Axton's obsessional relationship with language.]

The Names is language obsessed. Jim's estranged wife, an archaeologist's assistant, shuts down communication by resorting to an exclusive childhood jargon; their erudite friend Owen Brademas is a compulsive language collector; a spate of cult killings prove to be reactions against the tyranny of the alphabet. The limitations of dialogue are a frequent subject of conversation. Yet much of the novel is dialogue, philosophical in content and painstakingly rendered. The characters discuss language and its failure to order for them situations that seem increasingly disordered. Language is the net they seize upon in order to pull their experience neatly together, yet reality keeps escaping through the warp and weft—words no longer contain meaning, and no one speaker can contain all language. In the first pages of *The Names*, the reader is quickly frustrated by the aimless, apparently inconsequential dialogue as the characters, seeming as anonymous to us as their words appear empty, banter sleepily in the back of a Greek taxi after one of a series of high-powered business dinners:

> "I didn't know you were so deep," she said.
> "I'm not normally."
> "You've clearly studied the matter.... We need a Japanese monk." (5)

Yet, as Budge remarks gleefully in *The Day Room*, "Things come out in casual talk." In keeping with Mikhail Bakhtin's notion of polyphony, voices speak meaningfully only when placed in context with, or set in opposition to, other voices. Cumulatively, and in relation to one another, the silly speakers talk larger sense,

"You don't want to climb it because it's there," she said. "Lindsay cuts to the heart of things."

Yet, Jim must explore language more intimately before he can sift out the "heart" of language even amid such brittle, often desperate chatter. This intimate exploration takes place through direct, participatory encounters, more sustained conversational interactions than these elliptical fragments that begin the novel. Neither the reader nor Axton is yet prepared to make connections between these fragments. Yet, somewhat grudgingly, we are intrigued.

Interestingly, one character tells Jim Axton that his first name is also the name of an Arabic letter (144). DeLillo's characters themselves are, in fact, literal characters, hieroglyphs within the larger text of the novel. If DeLillo's characters can be considered letters whose synchronic combinings form words or utterances within a larger discourse whose subject, language itself, is self-reflexive, then Axton's own verbal encounters with other characters who are counterparts of himself can be seen as part of that ongoing dialectical inquiry whose subject, medium, and ultimate answer is language.

Like the rest of the characters, then, Jim Axton is subsumed by language. As his last name suggests, he perceives himself to be "acted upon," even "axed on," by a language system which refuses to fulfill its implied promise to define reality, let alone allow him to communicate with others to his satisfaction. Jim's job mirrors his situation—he is a "risk analyst" for a nameless multi-national corporation that insures governments against terrorist attacks, terrorism probably sanctioned by the self-same corporate empire. The corporation is itself an oppressive construction, that mutates words to suit its purposes—Jim soon realizes that the term "risk analyst" is every bit as oxymoron as "military intelligence." (He realizes he has been "engaged in a back-channel dialogue with the CIA" and resigns.) Jim seeks expression, connection, and satisfaction through language, not repression of individuality in exchange for false security. His willingness to play government pawn co-opts not only his humanity, but his language as well: once a freelance writer, he now sends telexes.

At the beginning of *The Names*, it is apparent from his hyper-awareness of words that Jim has already realized that the system under which he operates is made of language. He then attempts, like a double agent, to work within the very system he hopes to overturn, by examining the workings of its grammar. His progress through the novel is thus a movement away from an entrapment within language, toward a realization that words, despite their ancient origins, can be regenerated within himself. He can recombine the elements of discourse into new utterances that satisfy rather than oppress. Language is a mutable medium, not a monument, a manmade offering rather than the temple itself. "This is what we bring to the temple, not prayer or chant or slaughtered rams. Our offering is language" (331). However, before he can make that offering, he must acknowledge its artifice. Through his examination of language, in the form of a series of increasingly direct conversational encounters with characters we perceive as the "Others" of Foucault's discourse, he sees not only language's artifice, but how people have forced it to function as a protective construction to shield them from doubt, and thus from direct experience as well. The option for freedom, Jim discovers, likewise comes from language.

The danger of demanding that language recreate a single, arbitrary reality is brought home to Jim in emphatic terms during a disturbing interchange with a member of a cult responsible for a series of random killings. Andahl, who wears women's fleecy synthetic boots, belongs to an arcane sect of nomads bent on obeying the "letter" of their own grim law. They murder according to the initials of their victim's names, which in turn must match those of the murder locale—this schema in order to attempt the binding of symbol and object into one-to-one correspondence through a terminal act of connection. "It had to be this one thing, done with our hands, in direct contact" (209). Threatened by the chaotic flux of existence, the killers superimpose uncertainty with pattern, however arbitrary and destructive, in an attempt to relieve their frustration over their own indeterminate destinies. Like the slogans they chisel on stone, their murders are chiseled expletives of defiance.

—Paula Bryant, "Discussing the Untellable: Don DeLillo's *The Names*." *Critique: Studies in Modern Fiction* 29, no. 1 (Fall 1987): pp. 17–19.

[Matthew J. Morris's essays have appeared in *American Literary Realism* and *Contemporary Literature*. In this excerpt, Morris explores Owen Brademas' archaeological ambitions as analogous to, and complicit with, the murderous ambitions of the cult.]

Owen's relation to the cult resembles our own relation to the novel as a whole: he seeks, at least at first, to satisfy his intellectual curiosity about it. Initially he finds it inaccessible, or, in other words, unreadable. His fellow investigator Jim elaborates the connection between reading and human relations when, having found a cult member willing to talk to outsiders, he realizes he must in fact have found an ex-cult member:

> Andahl etched an almost human face on this hard blank surface. How could he still be one of them? ...
> He'd told me those words on the rock were put there by someone leaving. The apostate manages his own escape by revealing a secret of the organization, breaking its hold on him. He was the one who'd painted the words. (216)

The frequent motif of faces in this novel usually marks a positive moment, since in studying faces we do a kind of reading with immediate human consequences. Unfortunately, many characters find that they can overcome the inscrutability of other people only by eradicating all differences between themselves and the others—that they can read the alien only by becoming one with him. Thus when cult member Avtar Singh concludes an informative discussion with Owen of the group's activities by saying, "You're a member now" (298), Owen cannot resist for long—Avtar gets the last word. And indeed, Owen satisfies his curiosity about the cult only at the price of complicity (failure to stop the final murder).

One might argue that Owen allows himself thus virtually to become a member of the cult because he can think of no other way to carry out his otherwise harmless inquiry. From this point of view he is just unlucky, in his old age, to fasten his studiousness on to one of the few subjects that could implicate him in a crime.

But I would like to suggest that some such criminal conclusion was always latent in Owen's inquiries that, divorced (in his mind) from any human context, they were bound sooner or later to lead him into some life-denying connection. He admits to Jim that he has lost interest in the worldly meaning of his pursuit:

> In my current infatuation I think I've abandoned scholarship and much of the interest I once had in earlier cultures....
> Now I've begun to see a mysterious importance in the letters as such, the blocks of characters. (35)

While this fascination with letters may seem harmless in itself, Owen uses it as an excuse to overlook the connection between his profession of archaeology and the larger issue of colonialism that so often accompanies it. For example, when he tells the story of the English explorer Rawlinson who paid a Kurdish boy to risk a fatal fall in order to copy a set of Babylonian letters, he virtually ignores Kathryn's suggestion that this story is "a political allegory" (80). On the contrary, he maintains, "it's a story about how far men will go to satisfy a pattern" (80)—as if pattern excluded rather than served politics.

Owen's final narrative, of his encounter with the cult at a place called Hawa Mandir and his failure to prevent the killing there of an old man named Hamir Mazmudar, contains further indications of the potential violence in reading. For example, the murderer Emmerich says to him:

> ... it's interesting that the word "book" in English can be traced to the Middle Dutch boek, or beech, and to the Germanic boko, a beech staff on which runes were carved. What do we have? Book, box, alphabetic symbols incised in wood. The wooden ax shaft or knife handle on which was carved the owner's name in runic letters....
> ... An alphabet of utter stillness. We track static letters when we read. This is a logical paradox. (291–92)

By now Owen's resemblance to the cult is obvious not only to us but also to him. In the remainder of this dialogue he seems almost nostalgic, for the cult will fall apart after its next murder.

But even when he tries to distance himself from the cult his connections to it assert themselves. Thus the childhood memory he substitutes for an account of the murder fails to secure him the sympathy, due to an innocent victim, which he seeks in narrating it. The subtext of reading-as-violence appears in this digression as inevitably as the return of the repressed.

Owen's memory arises when, preferring not to watch the murder, he spends the night in a silo. The silo reminds him of his boyhood in the Midwest, when he felt anxiety and isolation in a church full of rural folk (including his parents) who spoke in tongues. His inability to join in on that occasion so disturbed him that he fled the church room. When Jim introduces this digression—"In his memory he was a character in a story" (304)—we recall that Tap (who, as Jim and Kathryn's son, has seen a lot of Owen around the dig) has remarked that "Owen says 'character' comes from a Greek word. It means 'to brand or to sharpen.' Or 'pointed stake' if it's a noun" (10). These passages indicate that *character* as "blade" is implicit in Owen's study of written characters (letters), that on some level of consciousness he is always aware of a potential for harm in his studies, and that this potential is somehow related to the memory he narrates.

Indeed, the juxtaposition of Owen's childhood memory of farmers speaking in tongues with the recent murder in India implies that his isolation, paralysis, and flight in the face of the former is the cause of, or is at least psychologically resonant with, his weak and irresponsible reaction to the latter. Perhaps (since *post hoc* is conventionally *propter hoc* in narrative) his present interest in alphabets for their own sake, with no reference to the people who use them or the writing they constitute, this interest that has led him into complicity with a murder, stems from a wish to do something analogous to speaking in tongues and thus to recover the sense of community he lost on that distant day. A plausible scenario would have the young Owen increasingly seeking through archaeology the formal euphoria he could not attain through glossolalia.

—Matthew J. Morris, "Murdering Words: Language in Action in Don DeLillo's *The Names." Contemporary Literature* 30, no. 1 (Spring 1989): pp. 115–117.

DENNIS A. FOSTER ON THE PRELINGUISTIC TEXTURE OF WORDS

[Dennis A. Foster is Associate Professor of English at Southern Methodist University. He is the author of *Confession and Complicity in Narrative* (1987) and *Sublime Enjoyment: On the Perverse Motive in American Literature* (1997), as well as essays on modernist writers and pedagogy. In this excerpt, Foster explores language's physical texture as a consolation for the loss of reason in the novel.]

In my telephone book I find a separate listing for "CIA," as if they understand that many people who may want to contact them know only the acronym. As if they know that for aspiring informers the words "Central Intelligence Agency" say less about that fantastically uncentered, nearly autonomous disseminator of misinformation, paranoia, and terror than this trigrammaton: CIA. James Axton, first person narrator of Don DeLillo's *The Names*, calls the CIA "America's myth," suggesting its power to comfort and coerce as it sustains our culture. Particularly in its acronymic form, the CIA serves as a god, the One supposed to know the why and wherefore when all seems chaos to mortals. Like another acronymic name of god, the tetragrammaton YHWH, the letters screen, for believers, the unspeakable name. (To the Yahwist the letters mean "I am who I am": the name of God and the claim to being lie hidden and preserved in the same acronym.) The inconceivable bureaucracies, corporate conglomerates, and technological systems of our modern pantheon become both familiar and mysterious in their acronymic garbs.

The Names opens with James Axton commenting on his never having visited the Acropolis, the most visible and austere sign of Western civilization's first great flowering. It still evokes the classic gods—beauty, dignity, order, proportion—even while it is overrun with tourists. This "ambiguity ... in exalted things" touches the complex of desire, fear, and despair that runs through the book. Politics, economics, religion, and marriage have dimensions that seem transcendent even while they remain, like language, vulgarly physical. DeLillo's metaphor for this crossing of idea and flesh is the "cult" that Axton pursues throughout the book, a group devoted to a ritual of human sacrifice. What links the cult's members to the acronymic gods is their faith in an arbitrary, alphabetic system: the initials of their victims match those of the place names where the killings occur. The violence resulting directly from the cult's faith in its acronymic method is clearly insane, but it is only a step away from the violence flowing daily from the ABC's of contemporary business and government.

Most events in *The Names* take place around a group of foreigners in Athens: bankers, diplomats, businessmen, spies. James Axton, an insurance "risk analyst" and unwitting employee of the CIA, has given up working in the United States as a freelance ghostwriter to live in Athens near his son and estranged wife, an amateur archeologist. An air of witty desperation pervades these displaced people and their acquaintances, most of them just enough beyond youth to have seen failures of marriage, career, and purpose. David Keller, for example, having just married a second, much younger wife, pursues international banking as if it were commando warfare. Ann Maitland, married to a career diplomat, structures her peripatetic life through her love affairs in each of the cities she lives in. Owen Brademas, an archeologist, has abandoned anything like an academic life, narrowing his pursuits to finding and touching strange writings in stone. Having lost touch with conventional meanings in their lives, the characters multiply their motivations in order to arrive at rationales for understanding their lives.

Such diffusion of purpose should, one would think, lead to an attenuation of action. On the contrary, the characters fulfill their roles with an intensity that seems beyond the specific drives of the individual: Axton, for instance, succeeds as a spy in spite of himself. It is as if their actions address some unspoken, or even unspeakable need that their lives of work and language— whatever it is that makes them appear as distinct individuals— know nothing of. What DeLillo explores so remarkably in this book is the complicity between the physical texture of our daily, rationally pursued lives and the needs that persist from what I am calling a "prelinguistic" life. For it is when screens of reasonableness have evidently failed, as they have for James Axton, David Keller, and others, that we see how the work of culture is sustained by this physical texture, like the alphabetic density of words that persists when words cease to make sense. More like the cultists than they would like to believe, DeLillo's characters respond to something like alphabetic coincidences that have nothing to do with the apparent failure and nonsense of their lives.

"Abecedarians," the cultists call themselves, students of the alphabet, beginners. We were all abecedarians once, chanting our ABC's in a simple rhyme that imposes order on what is thoroughly arbitrary, tying our letters to one of our earliest songs. To sing the alphabet is to feel an order in our deepest verbal memories, and an ancient pleasure. "Something in our method finds a home in your unconscious mind. A recognition," one cultist says. He continues paradoxically: "We are working at a preverbal level, although we use words." Rather than preverbal, I would say prelinguistic, by which I want to get at a use of language that functions without symbolic representation. This unconscious "home," assuming it exists, is the brick and mortar, the absolutely familiar elements of life, but which can no longer be touched except through the structure of the house. Abecedarians reach toward that primal stuff of language.

—Foster, Dennis A. "Alphabetic Pleasures: *The Names*." *The South Atlantic Quarterly* 89, no. 2 (Spring 1990): pp. 395–397.

JOHN A. MCCLURE ON THE FINAL FRAGMENT OF THE NOVEL

[John A. McClure is Associate Professor of English at Rutgers University, New Brunswick. He is the author of *Kipling and Conrad: The Colonial Fiction* (1981) and *Late Imperial Romance* (1994). In this excerpt, McClure interprets the fragment from Tap's novel as an ironic statement of hope.]

By the end of the novel, though, Axton has had more than enough of conspiracy and, it would seem, its idioms. Before he leaves Athens, he makes a long-postponed visit to the Acropolis, and finds there examples of a strikingly different politics of discourse, resources for a different kind of romance. Axton's Acropolis is a place of congregation, free exchange, and "open expression," a language community antithetical in its purposes and principles of exchange to the conspiratorial community he is fleeing. "Everyone is talking," and the impression conveyed is one of rich heteroglossia, constructive dialogue, and catharsis. Even the stones seem to speak, and to instruct those who come to them in the purposes and powers of speech:

> I hadn't expected a human feeling to emerge from the stones but this is what I found, deeper than the art and mathematics embodied in the structure, the optical exactitudes. I found a cry for pity ... this open cry, this voice we know as our own.

Here are the resources for a very different kind of romance, one in which people come together to share knowledge, pain, and longing on a site resonate with history and with absence. This terrain—the half-empty temple, denuded of its divinities but still filled with suppliants, still ringing, albeit silently, with a "cry for pity" addressed to absent redeemers—resembles the space that Jameson designated in *The Political Unconscious* as the terrain of authentic romance in our time. It is one of the "abandoned clearings across which higher and lower worlds once passed," and which we still visit to remember older dreams of fulfillment and to confront our impoverishment. *The Names*, like *Running Dog*, depicts a kind of transgeneric quest, but one that ends more promisingly than Selvy's. And it repudiates, as *Running Dog* does, that version of history which would offer the intricate systems and conspiracies of postmodernity as adequate sources of wonder and transcendence. If romance has a home in the present, it is not within the machinery of capitalism, but in archaic and marginal places, like the Acropolis, where memory and desire bring people together to speak openly about what they have lost and what they want.

But the episode at the Acropolis is not the end of *The Names*. It is followed by a brief fragment from a novel, being written by James Axton's son, in which the young protagonist is attending a Pentecostal revival meeting somewhere on the American plains.

Here again there is a play of voices: the boy's parents and other worshipers are speaking in tongues, recreating that moment from biblical history when the spirit descended on the disciples and they began miraculously to speak in the different languages of the ancient world. But for the boy at least, this cacophony of voices is terrifying: he cannot understand, and, even worse, he cannot join them: "The gift was not his, the whole language of the spirit which was greater than Latin or French was not to be seized in his pityfull mouth." Fleeing the church, he finds himself in a bleak world without "familiar signs and safe places," but not without wonder. The last words of the fragment, and of *The Names*, describe the boy's reaction to this world: "This was worse than a retched nightmare. It was the nightmare of real things, the fallen wonder of the world."

I read this fragment as a second parabolic retort to the postmodern narrative that discovers romance in conspiracy, a counterhistory in which wonder survives the crisis of desacralization not by investing the mechanisms of multinational capitalism with all the power and mystery once ascribed to the forces of magicians and gods, but by facing the fact of our disinheritance, the emptiness of a world without God. And I imagine, even if DeLillo does not, the youngster fleeing toward the Acropolis, on his way to an encounter that will provide him with company and prepare him for the longer struggle, that of casting, in merely human speech, an image of the future as rich or richer than that which died with the gods.

—John A. McClure, "Postmodern Romance: Don DeLillo and the Age of Conspiracy." *Introducing Don DeLillo*, ed. Frank Lentricchia, (Durham, NC: Duke University Press, 1991): pp. 111–113.

THOMAS CARMICHAEL ON BELATEDNESS AND
SELF-REFLEXIVENESS

[Thomas Carmichael is the coeditor of *Constructive Criticism: The Human Sciences in the Age of Theory* (1995) and *Postmodern Times: A Critical Guide to the Contemporary* (*2000*), and is the author of essays on contemporary

American fiction, literary theory, and postmodern culture. In this excerpt, Carmichael discusses the problems with self-representation in the novel, through the cult's murders and Tap's novel.]

DeLillo's *The Names* is framed by James Axton's reflections upon the Acropolis. At the beginning of the novel the Acropolis is an intimidating site to be avoided: "So much converges there. It's what we've rescued from the madness. Beauty, dignity, order, proportion. There are obligations attached to such a visit" (3). At the end of the narrative, however, Axton finds himself wandering among the crowds at the Parthenon: "People come through the gateway, people in streams and clusters, in mass assemblies. No one seems to be alone.... Everyone is talking.... This is what we bring to the temple, not prayer or chant or slaughtered rams. Our offering is language" (331). But if this last rumination would seem to link the Parthenon with the city beneath it and to suggest a redemptive possibility for language, much of the narrative addresses a very different configuration in which language betrays an original absence that is the field of political violence, hegemony, and terror. Like *Libra*, *The Names* is presented as the product of an intertextual engagement at the levels of both story and discourse. Axton's son, Tap, is writing a novel about the early life of Owen Brademas, the novel's senior archaeologist, and a portion of this novel forms the final section of *The Names*. What is important about Tap's novel is its concern with the absence of transcendence, or what Tap calls "the nightmare of real things, the fallen wonder of the world," and the language of the narrative with its "spirited misspellings" that seem to intimate a compensatory desire to find, in Axton's words, "second and deeper meanings, original meanings" (339, 313). This tension in Tap's text between the desire for transcendence and the representation of its absence is also echoed in the preoccupation with film in *The Names*. Frank Volterra, the enigmatic director who assists Axton in his investigations into the novel's murderous cult, wants to film the cult in its act of ritual murder. In Volterra's view, the cult's mania is a response to a pervasive sense of belatedness, a sense of the always already represented nature of the world that is the condition of contemporary experience. As Volterra puts it, "This is where we are. The twentieth century is *on film*. It's the filmed century. You have to ask yourself if there's anything about us more important than the fact that we're constantly on film, constantly watching ourselves" (200). Although they exist entirely within DeLillo's text, both Tap's fiction and Volterra's proposed film function within *The Names* as intertextual intersections that signal the very absence and fear that the main narrative thread explores through the cult and its preoccupation with language.

The cult in *The Names* murders its victims by matching the victim's initials with the name of the place in which the intended victim happens to reside or into which he or she wanders. It is an abecedarian mania, and like the disaffected CIA plotters in *Libra* the cult members in *The Names* are ultimately engaged in a program of murderous self-reflexiveness. As Avtar Singh, one of its members, tells Owen Brademas, "The world has become self-referring. You know this. This thing has seeped into the texture of the world.... This is my vision, a self-referring world, a world in which there is no escape" (297). Avtar Singh anticipates what Win Everett in *Libra* will realize in his anticipation of Oswald's motives: "If the world is where we hide from ourselves, what do we do when the world is no longer accessible? We invent a false name, invent a destiny, purchase a firearm through the mail" (*Libra* 148). But for the cult, to murder is to signal a fundamental absence of significance in the world. As another cult member explains: "There are differences in meaning, differences in words. But know this. Madness has a structure. We might say madness is all structure. We might say structure is inherent in madness" (*Names* 210). These murders are a systematic mockery of the decentered and disseminated world of indifference in which the cult members live and which they associate with contemporary experience, and which the novel's intertexts associate with the very condition of writing as a generalized notion of discourse and with film as that which foregrounds the belatedness that is woven into the fabric of everyday life.

Belatedness and self-reflexiveness are the inescapable conditions of political violence in *The Names*, as they are in *Libra* and as they are in DeLillo's *Mao II*. In *The Names*, Axton reflects that "America is the world's living myth," and later he extends this view: "If America is the world's living myth, then the CIA is America's myth.... The agency takes on shapes and appearances, embodying whatever we need at a given time to know ourselves or unburden ourselves" (317). Axton's point is not, however, fundamentally different from the dilemma addressed by Avtar Singh, or from the tension generated by the self-represented intertexts in the novel. Ritual murder and political assassination, DeLillo's fiction repeatedly maintains, are always and also attempts to escape the prisonhouse of language, understood as all that which would undermine the illusion of an unmediated access to the real and the sound assumption of a coherent and stable subjectivity.

> —Thomas Carmichael, "Lee Harvey Oswald and the Modern Subject: History and Intertextuality in Don DeLillo's *Libra*, *The Names*, and *Mao II*." *Contemporary Literature* 34, no. 2 (Summer 1993): pp. 212–214.

MARIA MOSS ON THE MURDEROUS POWER OF LANGUAGE

[Maria Moss is the author of several essays that have appeared in *Amerikastudien: American Studies*. In this excerpt, Moss discusses the cult's aspirations toward godlike omnipotence through language control and murder.]

The cult members are language "connoisseurs" who respect nothing more than people's abilities with letters and words: 'How many languages do you speak'? is the sentence they utter when confronted with strangers. Owen Brademas is reminded of medieval guards at the city gate and wonders if his "entry depend[s] on the answer" (28). (As will become clear later, it indeed does.) The cult members claim not to be interested in "history, gods, tumbled walls, but only—and that makes them so fascinating to Owen—in "letters, written symbols, fixed in sequence" (30). Having dealt professionally with alphabets all of his life, Owen is drawn to the cult's unqualified fascination with letters and to their apparent "quest for originary language,

language that is immediate and immanent."[23] For the cult members, however, letters are no longer objects but subjects, causing them to kill endlessly.[24]

By surrounding their crimes with the aura of linguistic pursuit, the cult members apparently celebrate the "aesthetics" of murder. Yet, their desire to kill "aesthetically" is mainly indicative of the urge for added significance, since in a world devoid of meaning only death sets a mark, marks a place: "Crime induces a perverse kind of epiphany," Geoffrey Hartman maintains, "it marks the spot, or curses it, or invests it with enough meaning to separate it from the ordinary space–time continuum."[25] Singh, the cult's spokesman, seems to agree when he analyzes their reason for killing:

> The world for thousands of years was our escape, was our refuge. Men hid from themselves in the world. We hid from God or death. The world was where we lived, the self was where we went mad and died. But now the world has made a self of its own. Why, how, never mind. What happens to us now that the world has a self? How do we say the simplest thing without falling into a trap? (297).

Singh's complaint about the lack of mystery in the world, resulting in mankind's inability to hide from the world's (or God's) omniscience, also echoes one of Blumenberg's major concerns. Blumenberg favors a mythic universe, considering it both safer and less restrictive for mankind due to its obvious lack of anthropocentrism.[26] Yet, by trying to echo the prime significance of letters and languages and thus competing with the biblical dictum, "In the beginning was the Word, and the Word was with God, and the Word was God," the cult members create their own all-powerful universe. By proclaiming the superiority of the correct combination of letters, the cult members assume god-like authority over life and death, thereby actively preventing the creation of a mythic universe, that is, of an intelligible environment conducive to their desire for mystery.

Beyond and above the murders, the cult members acquire significance not—as may seem most plausible—by hiding themselves or by turning the killings into ominous experiences, but by hiding their name. By keeping their name a secret, they reach back to archaic rites that prohibit any mention of names for fear of being rendered vulnerable to enemies. For the cult members, language (that is, "letters fixed in sequence") is so alive that it is capable of killing.

NOTES

23. Weinstein 293.

24. Cf. Weinstein 303; he coins the term "subject not object" for the "airborne toxic event" in DeLillo's *White Noise*.

25. Geoffrey Hartman, "Literatures High and Low: The Case of the Mystery Story," *The Poetics of Murder: Detective Fiction and Literary Theory*, ed. Glenn W. Most and William W. Stowe (New York: Harcourt, Brace, Jovanovich, 1983) 201–29; 212.

26. My summary of "Gerade weil die Funktion des Mythos auf die Weltsicherheit des Menschen zentriert ist, ist der Komplex seiner Gestalten und Geschichten nicht anthropozentrisch" (Hans Blumenberg, *Arbeit am Mythos* [1979; Frankfurt/Main: Suhrkamp, 1990] 152).

—Maria Moss, "Das Schaudern ist der Meschheit bestes Teil": The Sublime as Part of the Mythic Strategy in Don DeLillo's *The Names*." *Amerikastudien: American Studies* 43, no. 3 (1998): pp. 489–490.

PLOT SUMMARY OF

Mao II

In an interview with Nora Kerr for the *New York Times Book Review* on June 9, 1991, DeLillo declares: "Not long ago, a novelist could believe he could have an effect on our consciousness of terror. Today, the men who shape and influence human consciousness are the terrorists." Such is one of the themes in DeLillo's *Mao II*, in which the novelist Bill Gray struggles with the loss of his artistic voice, and dies as he turns to terrorists to negotiate its return. Bill Gray allows his photo to be published for the first time, then dies anonymously; Abu Rashid, whose terrorism begins anonymously, ends up being captured on film by a world-famous photographer. This mirror-like narrative construction is one of the ways in which DeLillo's work embodies the ironies that proliferate self-representation in the postmodern world.

In the prologue section, entitled "At Yankee Stadium," Rodge and Maureen Janney try to spot their daughter Karen from among 6,500 couples being married by the cult leader Reverend Moon.

Part One begins as Scott Martineau, assistant to famous author Bill Gray, meets Brita Nilsson, a photographer, in a midtown hotel in New York City. Bill, a recluse who lives in hiding, has decided to allow his picture to be taken by this photographer of famous writers. Scott takes Brita to Bill's house, where she completes a photo shoot amidst desultory conversation. Bill admits he is tired of hiding and feels trapped, lamenting that he has been working on the same paltry book for 23 years. Brita brings a message from Charlie Everson, an old friend and editor of Bill's, instructing Bill to call him immediately.

Brita spends the evening with Bill, Scott, and Scott's lover Karen, who all live together in Bill's house. After dinner, Scott drives Brita back to the city. In the course of the evening, conversations and events reveal that Scott is a former fan of Bill's who tracked him down by working in the mailroom of Bill's publishing house, Karen is a former Moonie who escaped her deprogrammers and met Scott as she was meandering on the main street of a small Kansas town, and Bill is an uncontrollable drunk. That evening, Karen sleeps with Bill, as is their custom when Scott is gone, and Scott sleeps with Brita in her New York apartment.

Bill then goes to visit Charlie Everson in New York. Charlie reveals to Bill that a Swiss UN worker, who is also a published poet, is being held hostage in Beirut. Charlie wants Bill to participate in a press-covered event in London in which Bill reads the Swiss man's poetry and the hostage is released on live television in Beirut. Bill is skeptical and leaves. He sees Scott waiting for him outside the building but avoids him and escapes into the anonymity of the city.

As Part Two begins, Jean-Claude Julien, the hostage poet, is being terrorized by a boy who guards him. Both Jean-Claude and the boy are hooded. Meanwhile, Bill meets Charlie in London to do the press conference as requested. Charlie reveals that a Lebanese communist group is holding Jean-Claude. Following a phoned-in threat, a bomb explodes in the building where the press conference is to be held. The conference is postponed, and at dinner that night, a man named George Haddad approaches Bill and Charlie. He is a political scientist in Athens, the spokesperson for the Lebanese communist group, and the intermediary between those holding the hostage and those who want him released. George warns them that it will be extremely dangerous to hold their event, predicting that there will be a bomb in a very crowded area.

Brita is at an Andy Warhol art exhibit in New York and is approached by Karen, who is wandering in the city looking for Bill. Brita allows Karen to stay in her apartment while she is out of the country doing shoots. On her own in the city, Karen is drawn to the homeless population in Tompkins Square Park, and to a drug dealer there named Omar Neely. Karen brings food to the homeless and preaches Reverend Moon's message to them.

In London, George Haddad approaches Bill and proposes they work together secretly, without Charlie and the others. He wants Bill to come to Athens and meet the man responsible for keeping the hostage captive. In Athens, George tells Bill the man's name is Abu Rashid and explains that his Maoist-influenced group is seeking to create a Lebanon that transcends factional and religious differences, offering a classless, absolute being as a leader. Bill theorizes that terrorists and novelists are related in a precise and intimate way: "What terrorists gain, novelists lose.... The danger they represent equals our own failure to be dangerous.... Beckett is the last writer to shape the way we think and see. After him, the major work involves midair explosions and crumbled buildings. This is the new tragic narrative" (157).

Bill is hit by a car as he walks into the street. Bystanders gather to help him, but he refuses aid and walks away with a scraped face and internal injuries.

In Brita's apartment in New York, Karen watches television and sees a million people gathered in a great square, where in the distance is a portrait of Mao Zedong. She continues to administer to the homeless in the park and preach about a second coming and a universal family, replicating the voice of the Reverend Moon. To Karen's disappointment and jealousy, Omar stops dealing drugs in the park because he impregnated a girl.

In Bill's house, Scott organizes fan mail and makes lists compulsively. Meanwhile, Brita returns to her apartment in New York, where she and Karen watch the funeral of Ayatollah Khomeini on television. There are crowds of mourners numbering some three million. Devastated and unwilling to give the Ayatollah over to death, they beat themselves over the head until they are bloody, break through barricades, fall upon the dead body, parade it around, and throw themselves into the empty grave to keep the body out. Finally the body is buried in a metal casket and covered with concrete blocks. Karen is extremely disturbed.

In Beirut, Jean-Claude is becoming sick and delusional, wishing desperately that he could write something down. Outside his cell, the sounds of shells and Israeli jets indicate that war rages on. Meanwhile Bill, suffering from his injuries but unwilling to see a doctor, approaches four veterinarians he sees dining near him in a restaurant. He asks them for medical advice, claiming he needs it for a character he is creating in a novel. They conclude his "character" has a lacerated liver. Seemingly unaffected, Bill drinks with them all night and wakes up not remembering how he returned to his hotel. He has been writing about the hostage ever since he left London, and now he boards a ferry headed to Junieh, Lebanon, from which he plans to take a taxi to Beirut. He wants to find Abu Rashid, presumably in order to negotiate himself as a surrogate hostage. On the ferry to Junieh, Bill dies. A member of the cleaning crew finds him, says a prayer, and steals his passport and identification.

Karen returns to Scott at Bill's house, looking as distant as she did when Scott first met her. Brita has given her the contact sheets for her photos of Bill. Karen and Scott look over the sheets, and prepare for the possibility that Bill will never return.

In the last section, entitled "In Beirut," Brita has traveled to Beirut to photograph Abu Rashid for a German magazine. It is one year later. While she takes pictures of Abu Rashid, a hooded boy brings him his mail. All boys who work near him wear hoods in order to remain faceless. Abu Rashid tells an inquisitive Brita of his plans to build a new Lebanon, free of the Western threat and reliant on the absolute image of Rashid. He reveals that the hooded boy is his son, Rashid. When Brita asks him what happened to the hostage he took a year ago, he tells her he sold the hostage to the fundamentalists. Brita removes the boy's hood and takes a picture of him. The boy looks at her with extreme rage and attacks her, grabbing for the camera, but Brita defends herself. After a word from his father, the boy puts his hood back on and leaves.

Brita is staying in East Beirut. At 4 a.m., she hears noise and walks out on her balcony that overlooks the street. She sees a tank go by, escorting a wedding party. She toasts the newlyweds with a glass of melon liqueur. After all is quiet again, she sees intense white flashes in distance. At first she mistakes them for automatic weapons fire, but then she realizes that they are camera flashes, and watches as they assault the city.

LIST OF CHARACTERS IN

Mao II

Bill Gray is a famous, critically acclaimed author who has hidden himself from the press and the world for many years. Weary of being hidden, he allows photographer Brita Nilsson to take his picture for the first time and travels to London intending to participate in a press conference to help a poet held captive by a Lebanese terrorist group. There he is besieged by terrorist threats, injuries from being hit by a car, and his own alcoholism.

Scott Martineau is Bill Gray's live-in assistant. Once an ardent fan, he traveled to New York and learned the secret whereabouts of Bill's residence by working in the mailroom at the author's publishing house. Working together with his lover Karen, his life is entirely devoted to supporting Bill's writing, even after Bill's disappearance.

Brita Nilsson is a professional, gutsy photographer who is commissioned to take the first pictures of Bill that will ever be published. She spends a day and evening with Bill, Scott and Karen, after which she makes love with Scott in her New York apartment. A year after Bill's death, she is hired to shoot Abu Rashid for a German magazine.

Karen Janney is Scott's lover, discovered by him when she was wandering the main street of White Cloud, Kansas after joining the Moonie cult and escaping her deprogrammers. She is also Bill's lover, though she and Scott do not discuss it. When Bill disappears, she wanders through New York trying to find him and falls back into her cult beliefs, preaching Reverend Moon's message to the homeless.

Charlie Everson is Bill's former editor and longtime friend. He contacts Bill through Brita Nilsson and convinces him to come out of hiding for a small, exclusive press conference in London where he will read the poetry of a Swiss UN worker held hostage by a Lebanese terrorist group. Charlie's plan is foiled by terrorist threats and a bomb, and the two part ways in London when Bill disappears and travels to Athens.

George Haddad is a political scientist in Athens and a sympathizer of the Lebanese terrorist group. He serves as a mediator between the group and the people who want to free the Swiss hostage. In London, he convinces Bill to work exclusively with him and leave Charlie and his people behind.

Omar Neely is a drug dealer in Tompkins Square Park who becomes Karen's friend and lover. He leaves the park and Karen when he finds out that he impregnated a girl at Coney Island.

Abu Rashid is the leader of the Lebanese terrorist group who holds the Swiss UN worker hostage. He is both communist and Maoist in leaning, and he proposes to build a new Lebanon that retains its dignity by refusing Western influence and taking its identity from the image of Rashid.

CRITICAL VIEWS ON

Mao II

JEREMY GREEN ON PUBLIC AND PRIVATE SPACE IN THE NOVEL

[Jeremy Green is an Assistant Professor of English at the University of Colorado. In this excerpt, Green explores the complex relationship between subjectivity and crowd mentality consciousness as exemplified by the mass Moonie wedding at the beginning of the novel.]

Mao II sets its forebodings into a slogan: 'The future belongs to crowds' (16). This phrase is placed at the end of a charged description of a mass Moonie wedding, which forms the prologue to the novel, and strikes the portentous and minatory note that prevails for much of the book. This first sequence, entitled 'At Yankee Stadium', bears only an oblique relation to the novel's central narrative, but it forcefully establishes an apocalyptic tone, and introduces the extremes of disbelief and certainty with which the text will grapple. If the force of DeLillo's slogan is to be assessed, and its implications worked out, it is with the spectacle of the Moonie wedding that the analysis must begin. *Mao II* dwells at length on a number of contemporary crowds, including the spectators crushed in the Hillsborough disaster, the mourners at the Ayatollah Khomeini's funeral and the protesters at Tiananmen Square, but these sequences all fall to a greater or lesser extent under the shadow of the Moonie crowd. The novel invites the reader to see the mass-marriage as the image of an unthinkable future.

Such an invitation is, in a sense, an ironic inversion of this crowd's assigned purpose. The mass-marriage is not a characteristic crowd, since it does not gather in response to a particular occasion or strong emotion, but involves instead both theatrical and religious impulses. The ceremony serves to unite six and a half thousand couples as part of the global family of the Unification Church, and in so doing looks forward to the redeemed time when the whole world will be organised as just such a special kind of crowd. For the true believer this represents humankind's salvation. For the non-believer, seeing in the spectacle uniformity, repetition, credulousness, and the loss of selfhood, the mass-marriage conjures up a nightmarish picture of the future.

But the Moonie ceremony is also unthinkable in a more immediate and perceptual sense. Although it provokes many of the more obvious, commonplace responses—the Moonies are 'fuelled by credulousness', they reduce knowledge to 'a set of ready-made terms and empty repetitions' (7), they drill all individuality out of the faithful—the spectacle in Yankee Stadium proves very difficult to comprehend, moving the spectators both to awe and bewilderment, to astonishment and to a kind of affective confusion, an uncertainty about what to feel. The Moonie Karen's father Rodge, watching in the stands, is galvanized into frantic action: he announces his intention to find helpline numbers, to scour libraries and join support groups. Her mother, by contrast, appears to lapse into an inertia alleviated only by a sardonic heartlessness: she proposes they take in a play or a show. The parents in the stands make an effort to defuse the impact of the spectacle by taking photographs, 'snapping anxiously, trying to shape a response or organize a memory, trying to neutralize the event, drain it of eeriness and power' (6). Snapshots hold out the promise of an eventual understanding, even as they register a present incapacity. In part, the parents are struggling with the shock of seeing the familiar made strange. Rodge reflects: 'There is a strangeness down there he never thought he'd see in a ballpark. They take a time-honored event and repeat it, repeat it, repeat it until something new enters the world' (4). What kind of new thing is this? 'He works his glasses across the mass, the crowd, the movement, the membership, the flock, the following' (5). The enumeration of these near synonyms reflects an awareness of the different connotations they carry, and testifies to Rodge's inability to give a name to what he sees: '"crowd" is not the right word. He doesn't know what to call them' (4). What he sees, what he fails to name, is the many resolved into the one, multiplicity into unity, the conversion of the individual participants into a shaped whole: 'From a series of linked couples they become one continuous wave ... one body now, an undifferentiated mass' (3). This undifferentiated mass is 'turned into a sculptured object. It is like a toy with thirteen thousand parts, just tootling along, an innocent and menacing thing' (7). Unity appears in this simile as unthinking mechanical potency, the impassivity and motion of an automaton, an image of the human transformed through sheer number into the machine. The mechanical appearance the crowd assumes relates to what is perhaps its most alarming, unthinkable aspect—the way in which all that is cherished as intimate and private is rendered by the ceremony crudely formulaic and public. This, finally, is what 'knocks him back in awe, the loss of scale and intimacy, the way love and sex are multiplied out' (7). Rodge's awe stems from the difficulty of imagining a self constituted in such a public and collective fashion, a subjectivity devoid of any private space in which to formulate and express its inner needs. It is as if public space, or, more accurately, the space of the Unification Church, has collapsed into the private, subjective realm. The crowd erases particular identities, and implies a threat even to the identity of the spectators, who lose their cognitive and emotional bearings.

—Jeremy Green, "Last Days: Millenial Hysteria in Don DeLillo's *Mao II.*" *Essays and Studies* (1995): pp. 131–133.

Sylvia Caporale Bizzini on Bill Gray's Loss of Identity

[Sylvia Caporale Bizzini is the coeditor of *Reconstructing Foucault: Essays in the Wake of the 80's* (1994). In this excerpt, Bizzini explores Bill Gray's loss of, and attempt to regain, his authorial identity.]

Mao II is the story of a famous, much-admired writer who can no longer find a satisfying place in contemporary society; it is for this reason that he decides to hide while he tries to write his last book. The writer feels displaced as an intellectual, and his writing loses the capacity of representing his *chiaroscuro* in a world which is dominated by terrorism. Each character symbolises an aspect of a society which apparently has lost all unity but which, paradoxically, is moving in a single direction. The book that Bill Gray is writing is a text which, significantly, he thinks will never be finished:

The language of my books has shaped me as a man. There's a moral force in a sentence when it comes out right. It speaks the writer's will to live. The deeper I become entangled in the process of getting a sentence right in its syllables and rhythms, the more I learn about myself. I've worked the sentences of this book long and hard but not long and hard enough because I no longer see myself in the language.

Language does not give back to the writer the image of himself he was used to seeing. Bill has lost control of the grammatical structures and the lexicon ('On the stage of the text, no footlights: there is not, behind the text, someone active (the writer) and out front someone passive (the reader); there is not a subject and an object.') The situation that Bill is going through can thus be interpreted as the result of questioning the very idea of authorship. It is for this reason that Bill feels he is not capable of publishing his book; he cannot do it because he feels that it is not *his* writing any more. And the work of revision that he carries out day by day is absolutely useless: the text keeps on slipping from his grasp. And so Bill decides to leave his hiding place and agrees to be photographed by Brita, a professional photographer who only takes pictures of writers. He is slowly capitulating to the pressures of the outside world and he tells Brita so in these words: 'There's a curious knot that binds novelists and terrorists. In the West we become famous effigies as our books lose the power to shape and influence. Do ask your writers how they feel about this?' (*MII*, 41). In this quotation two ideas that will become the backbone of the novel appear: the relation between terrorists and writers and that between writers and images.

Why after so many years of isolation does Bill Gray decide to publish his photograph and not his book? As we already know, Bill has a conflictive relation with his novel, that is to say with the text he is writing. This text does not recognise him as the 'Author' but as somebody that Barthes defined as a 'white card' or as the joker. When Bill feels that he has lost his identity as a writer (and above all as a committed writer), what he desperately needs is another identity. The camera can give him what he needs at this moment, an image which is able to tell him that, in spite of everything, he still exists as Bill Gray, the writer. This is what Barthes writes in *Camera Lucida*: 'Now, once I feel myself observed by the lens, everything changes: I constitute myself in the process of "posing", I instantaneously make another body for myself, I transform myself in advance into an image'.

For this reason Bill gives up his privacy and agrees to be transformed into an image and, significantly, the person who does it is a woman photographer who left her previous field of research (in the poor outskirts of town) to devote herself to going around the world taking pictures of writers. Through her job the impossibility of writing is transformed into a collection of images of people who write:

> It took me a long time to find out what I wanted to photograph. I came to this country it's fifteen years. To this city actually. And I roamed the streets first day, taking pictures of city faces, eyes of city people, slashed men, prostitutes, emergency rooms, forget it, I did this for years [...] But after years of this I began to think it was somehow, strangely—not valid [...] Then you know what you want to do at last [...] I will just keep on photographing writers, every one I can reach, novelists, poets, playwrights. This is what I do now. Writers. (*MII*, 24)

> —Sylvia Caporale Bizzini, "Can the Intellectual Still Speak? The Example of Don DeLillo's *Mao II*." *Critical Quarterly* 37, no. 2 (Summer 1995): pp. 108-109.

ADAM BEGLEY ON BILL GRAY'S IRONIC DISAPPEARANCE

[Adam Begley is the author of *Literary Agents: A Writer's Guide* (1993) and has served as a contributing editor to *Lingua Franca* and the *Paris Review*, as well as the book editor of the *New York Observer*. In this excerpt, Begley explores the irony surrounding Bill Gray's death.]

There's a description in *Mao II* of the young Bill Gray—Bill before he went into hiding—that fits DeLillo remarkably well. The young Bill was "wary of the machinery of gloss and distortion, protective of his work, and very shy and slightly self-romanticizing." DeLillo is indeed shy, and deeply distrustful of literary celebrity—the publishers' marketing hype, the shallow stuff peddled in author profiles, the posturing of the writer as public sage, our cultural conscience personified. "It's best for me to work in some level of obscurity," he told me in 1992. "I feel more myself—like when I was working on my earlier books. Obscurity is my natural environment, it's where I'm most comfortable."

Obscurity also fits with his endgame idea of novel-writing. As he puts it in the *Paris Review* interview, "we need the writer in opposition, the novelist who writes against power, who writes against ... the whole apparatus of assimilation." Although he claims to see nothing heroic in his own stubborn attachment to the written word (he can't help himself, he's compelled to write), I suspect that he's not immune to the romance of the lonely, defiant writer; it feeds his dedication. Romantic and contrarian impulses work hand in hand: if everything in the culture argues against the novel, that's what DeLillo's going to make. If celebrity is the expected path, he'll find a detour. He chooses to set up shop on the far periphery, in the shadows—out of sight, but with a clear view of the center.

Like David Bell, the Bill Gray we meet in *Mao II* is an artist in exile. But there's nothing happy about his remove from the world, nothing comic about his immersion in work. It's a portrait shot through with despair. Here's Bill, author of two slim "modern classics," sitting at his typewriter:

> He looked at the sentence, six disconsolate words, and saw the entire book as it took occasional shape in his mind, a neutered near-human dragging through the house, humpbacked, hydrocephalic, with puckered lips and soft skin, dribbling brain fluid from its mouth.

Acute cultural pessimism has leached into Bill's bones and poisoned his working life. He can take no pleasure in writing. He is worse than blocked. He's exhausted, empty, defeated. Like David Bell and DeLillo himself, he preserves the draft pages of his work-in-progress, but in Bill's case it's all sinister compulsion; the manuscripts are stored in a specially outfitted basement, part crypt, part bunker. Worst of all, Bill is trapped, imprisoned by self-imposed exile. A recluse of the Pynchon/Salinger variety, he has not shown himself in public for decades. Although he makes witty remarks about his predicament ("When a writer doesn't show his face, he becomes a local symptom of God's famous reluctance to appear"), he no longer knows how to undo his vanishing act.

At this bitter juncture in his career, Bill is only too happy to pin his problems on the Zeitgeist. He reads the signs of the times and concludes that the culture is through with writers, that the novel's day is done. *Mao II* takes up where *Americana* left off: "In our world," says Bill, "we sleep and eat the image and pray to it and wear it too." David Bell might have trotted out that sentence. But this time around, DeLillo has broadened the scope of his inquiry. Though compact, *Mao II* offers a global outlook; it makes room for London bombings, the Lebanese civil war, the Ayatollah Khomeini's funeral, the Tiananmen Square massacre, and an encampment of homeless people in New York's own Tompkins Square Park. DeLillo is scanning the horizon for the next thing, trying to predict the shape of tomorrow's consciousness.

Bill argues that the writer's place has been usurped by the terrorist: "Years ago I used to think it was possible for a novelist to alter the inner life of the culture. Now bomb-makers and gunmen have taken that territory. They make raids on human consciousness." He formulates a neat equation:

> What terrorists gain, novelists lose. The degree to which they influence mass consciousness is the extent of our decline as shapers of sensibility and thought. The danger they represent equals our own failure to be dangerous.

The plot of *Mao II* is an acting out of this gloomy cultural prognosis. Bill graduates from staged disappearance to actual disappearance. He travels to Lebanon at the height of the civil war hoping to offer himself up as a terrorist group's surrogate victim, a kind of volunteer Salman Rushdie. But he dies along the way, an anonymous death on a Beirut-bound ferry. The irony of his mute inglorious end serves a double purpose: it cancels his melodramatic pretensions; and it reflects far better than the heroism of a successful hostage-swap, DeLillo's endgame philosophy. The novelist who dares to play a part on the world stage, who makes a bid to share the terrorist's top billing, is dead on arrival.

—Adam Begley, "Don DeLillo: *Americana, Mao II,* and *Underworld." Southwest Review* 82, no. 4 (1997): pp. 489–491.

RYAN SIMMONS ON THE COMMON GROUND BETWEEN
BILL GRAY AND THE UNABOMBER

[Ryan Simmons' essays have appeared in *Critique: Studies in Contemporary Fiction* and *Modern Fiction Studies*. In this excerpt, Simmons compares Bill Gray's attempt at self-representation with that of the Unabomber.]

Within the year of Theodore Kaczynski's capture, Warner Books published *Mad Genius*, a paperback account of what it termed (in the subtitle) the Unabomber "Odyssey" written by journalists from *Time* magazine. In a statement that echoes DeLillo's novel, Lance Morrow writes in the introduction to this book, "As that successful paranoid Mao Zedong once advised, 'Let a hundred flowers bloom. Let a hundred schools of thought contend'" (2). Morrow's point is that a "multicultural supermarket of bad guys" has caused contemporary American culture to be marked by paranoia. As Morrow sees it, this is both because many of the "available enemies," from feminists to fundamentalist Christians, engage in paranoia, and because the proliferation of enemies has made most Americans, regardless of affiliation, feel paranoid: "Paranoia may come in either tribal or private form" (2). The Unabomber, in this scheme, is seen as a paranoid who spreads his paranoia to others. The depiction of the Unabomber in the American media (of which *Mad Genius* is representative) is in many ways a response to the polyphony that Morrow sees in contemporary culture. It is an attempt to contend with the chaos perceived as inherent in the presence of many discourses, to invoke, in Foucault's words, "the principle of thrift in the proliferation of meaning" (274).

Perhaps unsurprisingly, the Unabomber himself, in the "Manifesto," is deeply engaged with the problem of acquiring a voice that can be heard amid the noise of contemporary culture. In particular, of course, the "Manifesto" is a response to the noise of technology. But the Unabomber also tries to make a statement, in his writings as well as his actions, about how the individual actor can make a difference. In a harsh condemnation of "leftists," for instance, he writes: "Art forms that appeal to modern leftish intellectuals tend to focus on sordidness, defeat, and despair, or else they take an orgiastic tone, throwing off rational control as if there were no hope of accomplishing anything through rational calculation and all that was left was to immerse oneself in the sensations of the moment" ("Industrial" 187). In other words, for the author of this statement, it is imperative to believe that "art" can overcome "despair," that an individual's works, through reason, can make a difference in the world.

Reason, however, has necessarily given way to violence in the Unabomber's view; and this change has come about because of the proliferation of discourses:

> Anyone who has a little money can have something printed, or can distribute it on the Internet or in some such way, but what he has to say will be swamped by the vast volume of material put out by the media, hence it will have no practical effect. To make an impression on society with words is therefore almost impossible for most individuals and small groups. [...] In order to get our message before the public with some chance of making a lasting impression, we've had to kill people. ("Industrial" 212)

To a startling extent, then, the Unabomber's thoughts on the acquisition of a cultural voice parallel Bill Gray's: the priority that, both believe, once was given to the rational, culturally valuable voice no longer exists, and so the only option for the consciousness that wishes to be heard is violence. The common ground between the Unabomber and Bill Gray is that both believe that words can no longer be influential in the way that direct action is. Both believe in the importance of words, but the Unabomber, unlike Gray, thinks (based on the above passage) that *acts* of violence might be able to draw spectators' attention back to the words themselves; Gray, when he decides to confront the terrorists himself at the end of *Mao II*, seems to have abandoned words altogether. Perhaps this explains why Gray, unlike the Unabomber, is unwilling to advocate or to use actual violence: Gray's ultimate decision is to sacrifice himself (emphasizing both the power and the destruction of individual consciousness) to bring about results, and does not constitute a mere attempt to intensify his language. By the end of *Mao II* Bill has abandoned his pursuit of authorship. The Unabomber, in contrast, differs from the "author" discussed in DeLillo's novel only in his use of literal, rather than figurative, violence.

Before elaborating the implications of this statement, it may be necessary to explore the Unabomber's relationship to the role of "terrorist" as understood by Bill and others. The Unabomber, as I have already suggested, is the violent actor whom Bill sees as a threat to authorship, the "bomb-maker" whose exploits draw attention away from more thoughtful statements. His reclusiveness corresponds to the facelessness of the terrorist threat in Bill's mind. Yet, as I also have tried to suggest, the Unabomber in many ways is Bill; that is, the Unabomber occupies the spot that Bill alternately occupies, fears he can no longer occupy, and, finally, chooses not to occupy. The Unabomber—both as he represents himself in writing and as he has been represented by the media—stands for individual consciousness. As much as anything, this implies what the Unabomber is not: he is not a group (regardless of his use of "we" and of his association of himself with the group "FC," which the FBI and, consequently, the media never pursued). And he is not foreign: nearly from the start, the perpetrator of the bombs was assumed to be an American.

Certainly, the Unabomber fits the definition of a terrorist as one who uses "fear-inducing violence for a political purpose" (Wright 4), which seems like a commonsensical approach. Yet the Unabomber is, as we will see, very much an author, which may simply mean that his words have attracted almost as much attention as his actions. Or rather, his words and his actions—his language and his life outside of language—have been rendered inseparable, so that his "Manifesto" isn't dismissed in the same way that the verbal statements of foreign terrorists are, while at the same time his comments don't exactly receive an "attentive" reading, either. The reception of the Unabomber's words and actions illustrate a paradox in American culture, one with which DeLillo is deeply engaged in *Mao II*. Those who have written about the Unabomber in the American press have found themselves unable to treat their subject as just another terrorist, while at the same time remaining, for obvious and not-so-obvious reasons, unwilling to admit that they are in fact treating him as just another author.

—Ryan Simmons, "What is a Terrorist? Contemporary Authorship, the Unabomber, and DeLillo's Mao II." *Modern Fiction Studies* 45, no. 3 (Fall 1999): pp. 687–689.

MARK OSTEEN ON THE NOVEL'S DIGITALLY PROCESSED
CHARACTERS

[Mark Osteen is the author of *The Economy of Ulysses:
Making Both Ends Meet* (1995) and *Magic and Dread: Don
DeLillo's Dialogue with Culture* (2000), and the editor of
White Noise: Text and Criticism (1998). In this excerpt,
Osteen argues that both Jean-Claude and Karen are
enmeshed in the electronic data that reproduce them.]

Part Two advances another argument about authority, one
illustrated by its introductory photograph—a mass of Iranians in
front of a huge photo of the Ayatollah Khomeini. That is, it
considers the appeal of totalitarian authority, manifest in
Khomeini, Mao, and the terrorist leader Abu Rashid. As the
novel moves out of Bill's hermitage into the larger world that
consumes him, it depicts (like *Players* and *White Noise*) its
characters' attempts to reauthorize themselves, to wrest control
of the story by consenting to or contesting the spectacular
authors who dominate the photos. Also as in *Players*, DeLillo uses
a series of narrative "dispossessions"—cinematic shifts from
character to character (Reid 27)—to stage a battle for control of
the narrative that mimics the larger struggle for "the future."
The framing photo, however, implies that the outcome is a fait
accompli: Khomeini's visage glares at us in an arrogant
proclamation of his victory.

Yet this part opens instead with another man in a small
room—the captured poet Jean-Claude—thus moving from a
voluntary hostage (Gray) to an involuntary one. At first full of
plans, Jean-Claude soon forgets them and begins to identify with
his captors (the so-called "Stockholm syndrome"). This
breakdown of his mental story ("there was no sequence or
narrative" to his days [109]) leads him to lose control over his
identity. Thus his hooded anonymity proves the authority of his
captor, whose invisibility imitates Joyce's godlike author. As Jean-
Claude's initials indicate, his role is to be a sacrificial victim, a
martyr to the same economy of authorship that destroys Bill. By
the end of the novel Jean-Claude, like *Libra*'s Lee Oswald,

becomes a character in somebody else's book, but remains unsure who the "author of his lonely terror" really is (111). He eventually becomes only a "digital mosaic in the processing grid" (112).

These scenes suggest that terrorist leaders generate a revolution in authorship and character: Jean-Claude is remade not of written words but of electronic bits. In this new mode of circulation, characters are disassembled, disseminated, and then reassembled by reporters, photographers, and cinematographers; authorship is no longer a matter of lonely individuals laboriously pecking out words on typewriters, but of invisible leaders giving orders and producing messages, which are then altered and relayed by the media and passed on to consumers. The final products are media events in which the messengers play a crucial "gatekeeping" role (Weimann and Winn 68): by selecting which stories get told, they collaborate in authoring the events. Both characters and audiences are thereby interpellated into the electronic mesh.

Karen represents such audiences, those individuals who imagine themselves in or as crowds. "Thin-boundaried" and permeable, she lacks a singular identity, instead acting as what Mark Edmundson calls a "conductor, a relay point [...] for currents of [penetrating] force" (108). She "believe[s] it all, pain, ecstasy," whatever floats through the airwaves; she both carries and transmits "the virus of the future" (119). When Scott first found her after her brutal deprogramming, he recognized her as "something out of Bill Gray" (77). But with Bill gone, she is a character in search of an author, and so travels to New York City, stays in Brita's apartment, and roams the streets around Tompkins Square Park, mingling with the homeless and disenfranchised. This city-within-a-city resembles the centerless, desperate crowd in the Sheffield photo, or, in a refrain that runs anonymously through the text, "it's just like Beirut" (146). To Karen, these people are just a "set of milling images with breath and flesh" (149), indistinguishable from the poor she has seen on TV. But she accurately grasps that this "life-and-death terrain where everything is measured for its worth" (151) constitutes a junkyard of capitalism crammed with the leftovers of America's consumer paradise; as DeLillo elsewhere notes, these people exemplify the "consequence of not having the power to consume" (qtd. in Nadotti 93). Nevertheless, capitalist images retain a vestigial presence here, for example, in the youthful drug-dealer Omar's Warholian T-shirt, with its rows of Coke bottles; in his attempts to sell marijuana; in the shopping carts full of meager possessions; in the "homes" made of discarded TV boxes. If, as DeLillo shows in *Americana*, to consume in America is to dream (270), these are people whose dreams have been stolen or lost. And dreams are what Moon and other spectacular authors promise to give them back.

While immersing herself in the lives of these lost souls, Karen also studies photographs of disasters, crowds, and holy men. Watching a Tiananmen Square demonstration on TV, she understands that it illustrates the "preachment of history" which pits "[t]he motley crowd against the crowd where everyone dresses alike" (177): the novel's argument about the future is staged as a TV show. A little later, Karen watches Khomeini's funeral on television, and imagines herself going "backwards" into the lives of the mourners, feeling their grief (188). "Here they come, black-clad, pushing toward the grave" (192): the echo of the novel's opening words solidifies the link between Moon's and Khomeini's authority. In both crowds, ancient rituals of community (marriage, funerals) have become media events. Karen understands the mourners perfectly—"the living do not accept the fact that their father is dead. They want him back among them" (189)—wondering if "we share something with the mourners, know an anguish, feel something pass between us, hear the sigh of some historic grief?" (191). As she did when watching the Sheffield disaster, here again Karen experiences Aristotle's pity and terror from televised images. No longer Bill's creation, she has become, like Jean-Claude, a character in a global electronic narrative, captured by a spectacular authority that extends beyond the nation, beyond the moment, even beyond the grave.

—Mark Osteen, "Becoming Incorporated: Spectacular Authorship and DeLillo's *Mao II.*" *Modern Fiction Studies* 45, no. 3 (Fall 1999): pp. 655–657.

JOE MORAN ON THE CULTURAL VALUE OF THE RECLUSIVE AUTHOR

[Joe Moran is the author of *Star Authors: Literary Celebrity in America* (2000) and *Interdisciplinarity* (2002). In this excerpt, Moran traces Bill Gray's attempted emergence from obscurity in the context of contemporary, postmodern culture.]

DeLillo's novel does raise the possibility that author-recluses might be valued precisely because of their supposed aloofness from celebrity—as Gray puts it, "when a writer doesn't show his face, he becomes a local symptom of God's famous reluctance to appear ... The image world is corrupt, here is a man who hides his face" (36). But this seems to work through a simple reversal in which Gray's reclusiveness becomes merely an inverted form of promotion, a move which centres around the figure of Scott. His obsessive and eventually successful attempt to penetrate Gray's inner sanctum (which even involves finding work as a mail sorter in order to locate the author's address), and his concern with what Benjamin would describe as the "auratic" origins of Gray's writing—his meticulous filing and cataloguing of the diaries, letters and manuscripts, and pride in "being part of this epic preservation, the neatly amassed evidence of driven art" (32)—seems to be an effort to get beyond Gray's image as a writer and reach the real "artist" underneath. Scott believes that Bill should not publish his novel, using his silence to demonstrate that, in a culture of pure simulation, "the withheld work of art is the only eloquence left" (67). But this concern with purity and essence seems to derive ultimately from an anxiety that Gray might diminish his stock of symbolic capital by undermining its rarity value. As Scott puts it: "Bill gained celebrity by doing nothing ... [he] gets bigger as his distance from the scene deepens" (52). With the help of a monthly check debited directly from Gray's account, Scott also proves an excellent custodian of the author's reputation after his disappearance at the end of the novel, releasing some of the pictures but leaving the manuscript where it is, "collecting aura and force, deepening old Bill's legend, undyingly" (224). Although Scott's motives are not primarily financial, there is still a sense that the author has been marketed for consumption—as though, as Stuart Ewen puts it in a similar context, "the critique has been turned on its head, packaged, and used against itself ... skinned and transmuted into a consumable style."[25] So the author-recluse represents here primarily an example of the media's ability to reverse the terms of celebrity and use the kudos attaching to artistic "integrity" to its own advantage. What is absent is a notion of the author-recluse as a contested ideological site, a pivotal point of contention in debates about the role of authors, the nature of fame and the relationship between cultural authority and exchange value in capitalist societies. As a cultural myth, then, the author-recluse is produced not simply by "the media" but by authors themselves (the fact that it is Scott who is using Bill in this way implicitly exempts the latter from any suggestion of creative self-invention) and their public.

Mao II's idea of cultural mediation as a one-way process, in which the celebrity author is merely the victim of an all-consuming publicity machine, is reinforced in the second part of the novel when DeLillo explores the relationship between writers, terrorists and crowds. Gray comes out of hiding at the suggestion of Charlie Everson, flying to London to speak at a reading aimed at raising awareness of the Beirut hostage's plight. The reading, however, is interrupted by a terrorist bomb, part of a botched plan to capture Gray and release Jean-Claude Julien simultaneously. Then, at the suggestion of an intermediary, George Haddad—and apparently tiring of the ways in which his celebrity name has been used to give publicity to both the campaign for the Swiss poet's release and the terrorists themselves—Gray makes his way to Lebanon to negotiate with Julien's captors in person. This extraordinary move springs from his frustration at being turned into a cultural commodity in spite of his best efforts at abnegation and denial, and his subsequent conclusion that his failure to be "dangerous" means that his life as a writer has been "a kind of simulation" (97). Gray's efforts to find a more active social role for the author are thus part of his belief that writers have become "famous effigies as our books lose the power to shape and influence"—only terrorists can now "alter the inner life of the culture," he laments, because writers have all been "incorporated" (41).

This comparison between writers and terrorists is, in fact, introduced only to be inverted at the end of the novel. Gray's plan to bring about the hostage's release ends in anticlimactic failure—he dies on a ferry on the way to Lebanon from internal injuries sustained during an earlier car accident—but in a way which undercuts this earlier notion of terrorists as unco-opted and instead promotes the writer as the last (albeit diminishing) hope for humanity. The Lebanese terrorists depicted in the novel's epilogue prove to be addicted to the image world, wearing a portrait of their leader, Abu Rashid, on their T-shirts, looking at videos of themselves taking part in the war, and apparently aiming to kill Bill, photograph the corpse and release the picture to the world's media whenever it will have most impact. In an age when "news of disaster is the only narrative people need," (42) terrorists who exploit the narrative and dramatic impact of television bulletins are the power-brokers, while authors like Gray are a hunted, dying breed—indeed. Brita describes herself at the beginning of the novel as undertaking a "species count" of writers (26), and at the end she gives up her project to photograph terrorists instead. But DeLillo's characterization of the broader social world which Gray fleetingly embraces suggests that the latter's inability to survive in this world indicates an admirable refusal to compromise. Only "the secluded writer, the arch individualist, living outside the glut of the image world,"[26] it seems, remains untainted by postmodern culture—and only then by retreating from it into silence.

NOTES

25. Stuart Ewen, *All Consuming Images: Style in Contemporary Culture* (New York: Basic Books, 1988), 99.

26. DeLillo quoted in Adam Begley, "The Art of Fiction cxxxv: Don DeLillo," *Paris Review*, 128 (1993), 296.

—Joe Moran, "Don DeLillo and the Myth of the Author-Recluse." *Journal of American Studies* 34, no. 1 (April 2000): pp. 145–147.

JEFFREY KARNICKY ON THE SIMILARITIES BETWEEN THE
NOVEL AND ANDY WARHOL'S ART

[Jeffrey Karnicky teaches at Pennsylvania State
University. In this excerpt, which considers Brita
Nilsson's encounter with Warhol's art, Karnicky argues
that DeLillo and Warhol share an acute awareness of the
proliferation of repeated images in popular culture.]

Andy Warhol appears in two of Don DeLillo's novels, *Mao II* and
Underworld. *Mao II* takes its title from a Warhol silkscreen that
also adorns the cover of the novel; in the novel, DeLillo's
characters look at Warhol's work in museums and offer theories
about the work's power. Warhol is less of a factor in *Underworld*.
He appears only once, in the chapter describing Truman
Capote's Black and White Ball—"Andy Warhol walked by
wearing a mask that was a photograph of his own face" (571)—
but this brief appearance highlights some important connections
between Warhol and DeLillo. This image of Warhol's image,
doubled in the photograph yet obscured by a mask, recalls many
similar instances in DeLillo's fiction. From the film of Hitler
impersonating Charlie Chaplin's "Great Dictator" in *Running
Dog* to the discussion of "the most photographed barn in
America" in *White Noise*, DeLillo's novels are interested in the
ways that image proliferation, often engendered by filmic,
televisual, or photographic repetition, affects our conception of
the world. (...)

Both Warhol's art and his writing draw attention to the power
of repetition as it relates to words and images, a power that is
central to DeLillo's fiction on many levels. DeLillo's recent
novels function almost as a casebook of strategies for engaging
the unavoidable and undeniable proliferation of images in
contemporary American society. Such strategies are multivalent;
DeLillo's novels, like Warhol's art, are not a critique of the
endless precession of simulcra, of images distanced from their
origins, but are instead deeply informed and influenced by the
ways in which the repetition of images has become
commonplace. In other words, in the worlds of DeLillo's fiction,
image proliferation is neither mourned nor celebrated; it is
strongly established as a matter of fact that cannot be ignored, as

a creative force to be actively engaged. A character in *Mao II* rhetorically asks, "Isn't there beauty and power in the repetition of certain words and phrases?" (62). Warhol and DeLillo share an interest in the conditions and effects of this "beauty and power." Both are concerned with the media that allow the repetition of words and images: the tape recorder, the camera, the television. Likewise, they both investigate the ways that these forms of mechanical reproduction are intimately intertwined with the creation of subjectivity.

Warhol's photographic mask of his own face illustrates how the proliferation of an image can render subjectivity. He stands out as a guest at the costume ball because, even with, or because of the mask, everyone knows who he is, precisely because he is nothing more or less than his image. There's nothing else there. He himself says, "some critic called me the Nothingness Himself and that didn't help my sense of existence any. Then I realized that existence itself is nothing and I felt better. But I'm still obsessed with the idea of looking into a mirror and seeing no one, nothing" (Warhol 7). Because of this "nothingness," Steven Shaviro argues that "the 'real' Warhol never appears; all we see is a mask, but there is nothing behind the mask" (Shaviro 205). Likewise, there is "no one" behind the mask. Warhol exists as the iteration of his own face in the photograph. The guessing game as to who's who behind the masks is irrelevant. Warhol is the photograph and the face; both are pure surfaces with nothing to interpret. No lost referent exists; the face becomes a repetition of the photograph as the photograph becomes a repetition of the face. Neither precedes the other. Much like Warhol's art, his face is a product of seriality; behind every image one finds another endlessly repeatable image: 210 Coke bottles, 100 dollar bills. Warhol is indeed "no one"; his "existence" as "nothing" is an effect of the serial repetition of his image.

So what can one say about Warhol if he and his work are nothing but an endless repetition? Brita Nilsson, the woman who photographs Bill Gray in *Mao II*, looks at a "Warholish" painting of Mikhail Gorbachev, called *Gorby I*, and is overcome by Baudrillardian melancholia:

> Brita wondered if this piece might be even more Warholish than it was supposed to be, beyond parody, homage, comment and appropriation [...] she thought that possibly in this one

picture she could detect a maximum statement about the dis-
solvability of the artist and the exaltation of the public figure,
how it is possible to fuse images [...] and to steal auras, Gold
Marilyn's and Dead-White Andy's and maybe six other things
as well. Anyway it wasn't funny. (134)

Nilsson shares Baudrillard's fears in the face of the Warholian
image. With this "maximum statement," any hopes of recovering
original auras are eradicated. Images cease to mean anything at
all. As Nilsson notes, "there were six thousand Warhol experts
living within a few square miles of this gallery and all the things
had been said and all the arguments made" (134). For Nilsson,
Warhol's work has been worn out by so much critical attention.
There is simply nothing left to say; the work, in a sense, is dead.
Still, as a Karen Janney notes in *Mao II*, Warhol never seems
wholly dead; "he didn't seem dead because he never seemed real"
(62). And the entirety of chapter 8 in Warhol's *Philosophy*,
"Death: All About It," reads "I don't believe in it, because you're
not around to know that it's happened. I can't say anything about
it because I'm not prepared for it" (123). Warhol's work is not
grounded in a deathward logic of completion; the possibility of
recontextualization is always there.

—Jeffrey Karnicky, "Wallpaper Mao: Don DeLillo, Andy Warhol,
and Seriality." *Critique: Studies in Contemporary Fiction* 42, no. 4
(Summer 2001): pp. 339, 340–341.

PLOT SUMMARY OF
Libra

Libra is a fictional account of the assassination of President John F. Kennedy. As DeLillo writes in his "Author's Note" at the end of the novel, this single event has given rise to myriad facts, rumors and theories, none of which his novel pretends to render intelligible. Instead, DeLillo recreates the theoretical labyrinth by offering an intricately woven plot that, like the assassination theories, becomes entangled upon itself. The novel, like the JFK assassination, tells us more about the configuration of information we call history than about the event itself.

In *Libra*, two major strands of plot weave around each other. One plot concerns the conspiracy to shoot President John F. Kennedy and follows the maneuverings of Walter ("Win") Everett Jr., a semiretired CIA agent, and his former colleagues Laurence Parmenter, T.J. ("T-Jay") Mackey, and David Ferrie. The other plot is a narrative of Lee Harvey Oswald's life. In addition, two minor narratives add complexity and depth to the story: the intermittently placed interior monologue of Marguerite Oswald, Lee's mother, who addresses her words to "your honor"; and the inner musings of Nicholas Branch, senior analyst of the CIA, who has been hired to write a secret history of the assassination of President Kennedy and is overwhelmed by the mountains of information before him.

Part One begins with Lee's childhood in the Bronx borough of New York City, where he lives with his mother. Lee amuses himself with the "world inside the world," riding the subway trains for hours at a time, reading Marxist literature, and memorizing the Marine Corps manual on deadly force.

The narrative then moves ahead to April of 1963 and into the mind of Win Everett. Win has teamed up with Laurence Parmenter, T-Jay Mackey, and David Ferrie, former colleagues who were part of an elite CIA group called Leader 4. All four were reprimanded by the U.S. Government for running their own private anti-Castro operation at Coral Gables, resulting in their diminished status in the Agency. Win rallies them into a conspiracy to stage an attempted assassination of JFK by Cuban exiles, and brings in Guy Banister, a former FBI agent and private detective in New Orleans who mobilizes anti-Castro groups from 544 Camp Street. They want to punish President Kennedy for not destroying Castro, and for secretly commiserating with communist Cuba and Russia. Win wants to make it look like Castro retaliated against Kennedy for plotting Castro's death, and he has decided to use Lee Oswald, a former defector to Russia, to do the job.

Meanwhile the reader follows Lee from his childhood until age of 17, where he has joined the Marines, is an avowed anti-capitalist, and is looking to defect to Russia and join the socialist cause. Stationed in Atsugi, Japan, he meets a socialist named Konno, to whom he reveals classified information about American U-2 spy planes. After Japan, Lee travels to Moscow, where he reveals the same information to Russian authorities, surrenders his U.S. citizenship at the American Embassy, and attempts to kill himself when he finds he cannot get a visa to stay. He is followed by the KGB, specifically agent Alek Kirilenko, who pities him and gives him an Identity Document for Stateless Persons. Alek sends Lee to Minsk with a steady income from the Red Cross.

In New Orleans, Wayne Elko, a mercenary, pays a visit to Guy Banister looking for work; and David Ferrie, who works for Banister, goes to see Carmine Latta, a mafia man in charge of casinos, betting parlors, and drug traffic in Louisiana. Ferrie obtains cash from the Batista-nostalgic Latta to fund their scheme. Win Everett finds out that after Lee's return from Russia, he disappears from Dallas and takes a job working in Guy Banister's office in New Orleans, while passing out pro-Castro pamphlets on the street. Everett sends T-Jay Mackey to ransack Oswald's home, and uses the information Mackey finds to create a partly factual, partly manufactured, file and history on Oswald.

In Minsk, "Alek," as Lee now calls himself, marries a Russian girl named Marina. Marina becomes pregnant, and while the two wait to receive clearance to move to the United States, Oswald writes about his experiences in Russia. He saves the papers and smuggles them into the United States.

As Part Two begins, T-Jay Mackey, who believes that the assassination attempt should be real and not staged, develops a mistrust of both Parmenter and Ferrie. He wants to take over the conspiracy. Lee and Marina have moved to Fort Worth, Texas, where Lee is visited by George de Mohrenschildt, who on behalf of the CIA's Mark Collings offers to get him a job doing classified work in exchange for access to his writings on Russia ("the Kollective"). His marriage to Marina becomes tumultuous and he beats her, then separates from her, hiding out in Dallas. Here he runs into Bobby Dupard, the man whom he shared a cell with while in detention at Atsugi. Both conspire against General Ted Walker, an extreme right-winger bent on killing communists and blacks; Lee shoots at the General as he sits by the window in his home one night, but misses.

In the bayous west of New Orleans, T-Jay Mackey's sequestered training camp for anti-Castro guerrilla fighters includes Wayne Elko, David Ferrie, the Cuban exile Raymo, and "Leon" (Oswald). Meanwhile, Frank Vasquez, a Cuban compatriot of Raymo who taught grades 1-6 during Batista's reign and saw the communist uprising and coup, delivers a message to T-Jay from "Alpha 66": a major operation is being planned for November 18 in Miami. Vasquez speculates that the operation entails killing the president, and Mackey agrees to put every effort into it.

Lee moves to New Orleans with Marina and begins handing out "Fair Play for Cuba" pamphlets on the street. FBI agent Bateman, enlists him to pose as an anti-Castro and obtain a job with Guy Banister. Lee will draw pro-Castro revolutionaries with his pamphleteering and pretend to be an informer for Banister, while in reality he is an informer for the FBI against Banister and his "Alpha 66" group, which makes hit-and-run attacks on Soviet ships in Cuban ports.

Through Guy Banister, Lee meets David Ferrie, who takes him to meet Clay Shaw. Upon learning the date of Lee's birthday, Shaw declares him a Libran, which is the sign of the scales. Ferrie understands the significance of Lee's astrological sign: there is no knowing which way Lee's scales will tip, since Lee is working for both pro-Castro and anti-Castro groups. Lee's only wish is to go to Cuba and be a military advisor to Castro, and he will do whatever is necessary to achieve this end.

Jack Ruby, a Dallas strip club owner with mob ties, is heavy in debt and tries desperately to get a loan from Carmine Latta via his driver Tony Astorina. Astorina declines the loan but informs Ruby that Kennedy slept with mob boss Momo Giancana's girlfriend for two years.

Guy Banister plans to have Oswald shoot Kennedy in Miami. Meanwhile, T-Jay Mackey and Raymo develop a plot to foil Banister by leaking the Miami plans out so that the President will not hold a motorcade parade there. Mackey's plan is to do the shooting in Dallas, and then kill Oswald.

Lee arrives in Dallas and takes a job at the Texas Book Depository as an order filler. Mackey persuades Lee to carry out the assassination by offering him passage to Cuba. After Lee shoots from the Book Depository, he is to go to a movie house and wait there in the theater for Mackey to facilitate his transport to Cuba. Mackey's real plan is to use Oswald as a scapegoat and have his own men's crossfire kill the president.

When the President arrives in Dallas and heads down Elm Street on the parade route, Lee hits him with one bullet from the Book Depository and Raymo finishes the job from the grassy embankment by hitting him with an exploding bullet to the head. Raymo escapes by car while Lee shoots a policeman who tries to detain him and is then jailed. As he is being transferred to the county jail, Jack Ruby shoots and kills him, as planned by mafia boss Carmine Latta, for which he receives $40,000.

The story ends on the day of Lee's funeral. Marguerite, his mother, begins to doubt whether Lee ever really belonged to her and wonders how far back the government began to conspire to use him. She takes comfort in the thought that at least they cannot take away the power of her son's name.

Libra

Lee Oswald is the son of Marguerite Oswald. From a young age, he sympathizes with the socialist cause and dreams of living in a socialist state such as Russia or Cuba, where he can contribute his talents to further the anti-capitalist cause. In exchange for passage to Cuba, where he wishes to serve as a military advisor to Castro, Lee shoots President Kennedy. Duped by the anti-Kennedy conspirators, Lee is arrested and shot dead by Jack Ruby.

Marguerite Oswald is Lee Oswald's mother and raises her son largely by herself, frequently moving from city to city and working long hours away from home. She speaks an interior monologue in which she addresses "your honor" intermittently throughout the novel, arguing her son's innocence and resourcefulness.

Nicholas Branch is a senior analyst of the CIA who has been hired to write a secret history of the assassination of John F. Kennedy. Only a select few know of this project, and he is receiving his information from the Curator of the Historical Intelligence Collection of the CIA. As his research progresses, Branch feels more and more as if he is being swallowed by the mountains of information that pile up in his office and in his head. Branch is perhaps a version of DeLillo himself.

Marina Prusakova Oswald is Lee's wife, whom he met in Russia during his stay there. After they move together to the United States, the marriage becomes more and more strained and Lee begins to beat her. After the assassination and Lee's death, Marina officially admits to her husband's guilt in exchange for a house, something Lee could never give her.

Alek Kirilenko is the KGB officer in Russia who follows Oswald during his stay there. Oswald gives him all the information he has on the American U-2 spy planes over Russia. Despite Oswald's dyslexia, emotional instability, and seemingly delusional nature, Alek takes a liking to the young man and allows him to stay in Russia with an Identity Document for Stateless Persons.

Walter "Win" Everett Jr. is a semiretired CIA officer who was once part of an elite group called Leader 4. He calls his former Leader 4 colleagues together and plans to stage an attempted assassination on JFK in Miami. Win decides on Oswald as the killer and creates a file on him that will incriminate him after the fact. Win's plan is overtaken by T-Jay Mackey, who wants the President killed rather than stage a fake assassination attempt.

David Ferrie was one of Win Everett's former colleagues in Leader 4 and at Coral Gables. He is a professional pilot and amateur cancer researcher who once wanted to be a priest but was defrocked for pedophilia. Ferrie works with Guy Banister in New Orleans and helps to orchestrate the assassination, serving as a pilot and a liaison between Oswald, whom he befriends, and the men who want to use Oswald as a staged killer.

Laurence "Larry" Parmenter was one of the former Leader 4. He works with Win Everett to generate and implement the plot to stage an attempted assassination on President Kennedy.

T.J. "T-Jay" Mackey was one of the most adept members of the CIA's Leader 4, and a veteran field officer. He was also reprimanded for the Coral Gables affair, but is the only one who refused to sign the letter of reprimand. He helps to implement Win's plan to stage an assassination attempt on JFK, but decides to foil the plan in Miami and work secretly with Raymo and Frank Vasquez to kill the president.

Raymo is an anti-Castro Cuban exile and a close friend of T-Jay Mackey. He provides the sharpshooting for the Kennedy assassination, firing an exploding bullet that hits the president in the skull.

Frank Vasquez is an anti-Castro Cuban exile who works closely with Raymo and T-Jay Mackey on the assassination of JFK. He assists Raymo on the day of the assassination, providing him with his gun and driving the getaway car.

Wayne Elko is a mercenary soldier. In need of work, he contacts Guy Banister just as the Miami assassination attempt plans are beginning to take shape. T-Jay trains him with the others, but abandons him when he decides to secretly move the plan to Dallas.

Guy Banister is a private detective in New Orleans who spent 20 years in the FBI and was the superintendent of the New Orleans Police. His office on 544 Camp Street is the nerve center of the anti-Castro operations in the United States. Banister works on the plan to stage an assassination attempt in Miami, but that plan is foiled by Mackey.

Jack Ruby is a strip club owner in Dallas who once worked for Al Capone in Chicago. He is addicted to Preludin and is in staggering debt, for which he tries desperately to get a loan without success. Ruby agrees to shoot Lee Oswald for Carmine Latta, a mob boss, in exchange for the immediate cancellation of a $40,000 loan.

CRITICAL VIEWS ON

Libra

FRANK LENTRICCHIA ON THE NOVEL'S DOUBLE NARRATIVE

[Frank Lentricchia's books include *The Gaiety of Language* (1968), *Robert Frost: Modern Poetics and the Landscapes of Self* (1975), *After the New Criticism* (1980), *Criticism and Social Change* (1983), and *Modernist Quartet* (1994). He is also the editor of *Introducing Don DeLillo* (1991). In this excerpt, Lentricchia compares the novel's two plots: the conspiracy to shoot John F. Kennedy and the narrative of Oswald's life.]

One of *Libra*'s more uncanny effects is anachronistic: DeLillo's wager is that we will read his book out of the political history that Watergate and Iran-Contra has made, as if Watergate and Iran-Contra preceded 22 November 1963, as if the novel's narration of the events of twenty-five years past made that day in November contemporaneous with its retelling. *Libra*'s politically caustic and unsettling point is therefore inextricable from DeLillo's effort to focus our culture's interpretation of its political history through the lens of post-Watergate America, so that even the reader inclined to believe that Oswald acted alone, but now grown accustomed to rogue government conspiracies of anti-Soviet demonologists, American intelligence, and multinational business and criminal interests, will be likely to grant DeLillo that the CIA, the Mafia, and the Cuban exile community in Miami, either individually or in concert, possessed sufficient motive and resources to plan and execute the murder whether or not they in fact did so. As hatched, the plot is not to kill the president but to lay down fire on the street, to stage a spectacular miss. But as the operation moves from theory to execution it passes into the hands of one T. J. Mackey, a CIA agent who is also a Bay of Pigs veteran, and his Cuban recruits, the shooters who are supposed to be actors but whose politically triggered passion for revenge, like Mackey's, turns assassination theater, the representation of violence, into the real thing—the violent lurch backward, exploded brain tissue, and the dead who persist through history's ambiguities.

DeLillo builds his conspiracy plot with relentless inevitability, making good on the original plotter's theory that all plots tend deathward. The Oswald plot, on the other hand, is so utterly episodic in character that it couldn't be approved by Aristotle, much less by the conspirators; it certainly doesn't deserve to be called a "plot" in DeLillo's senses of the word. What he has done in *Libra* is given us one perfectly shaped, intention-driven narrative while folding within it, every other chapter, a second narrative, his imagined biography of Oswald, a plotless tale of an aimless life propelled by the agonies of inconsistent and contradictory motivation, a life without coherent form except for the form implied by the book's title: Oswald is a "negative libran, somewhat unsteady and impulsive. Easily, easily, easily influenced. Poised to make the dangerous leap." DeLillo writes that Oswald "wanted to carry himself with a clear sense of role." But who is this "he" who wanted a "role," just who is it that stands in the wings waiting for a part in the theater of self? It doesn't much help to say that he is someone named "Oswald" who can get up from a chair where he's been reading a book, calmly walk over to his wife, pummel her with both fists, then return to the chair and resume his reading, quietly. The identity of the negative libran is the nonidentity of sheer possibility—of the American who might play any part. The negative libran is an undecidable intention waiting to be decided. And astrology is the metaphor in *Libra* for being trapped in a system whose determinative power is grippingly registered by DeLillo's double narrative of an amorphous existence haphazardly stumbling into the future where a plot awaits to confer upon it the identity of a role fraught with form and purpose.

The double narrative virtually forces us to read in order to catch up with the future; in order to find out how the drifting episodes of Oswald's life in the 1950s and early 1960s will be gathered on 22 November 1963 into the rigors of causality; in order to give Oswald's life everything that it lacks and that the conspirators' plot has: the literary wholeness of a beginning, middle, and end. We find ourselves seduced into reading with the hope of seeing Oswald made into a product of an environment in which paranoia is a reasonable response to the structure of the world. The original plotter (one Win Everett) sees himself as something of a novelist/playwright who has scripted a fiction, one of whose characters was an illusory lone gunman, a man of paper who a trail of carefully planted clues would lead authorities to conclude was real, that he was Castro's hit man, and that after the attempt on Kennedy's life had escaped to Cuba. The point was to get Castro blamed; Mackey's people would set up the play. The actual Oswald was irrelevant. But Oswald materializes as the real-life counterpart of a fictional lone gunman whose appearance almost turns history into designed narrative, almost makes believers of us all in astrology.

With his double narrative DeLillo toys with conventional political and novelistic expectations. He has written a book about the triggering event of our political paranoia in the context of a recent political scene which can only reenforce that paranoia. DeLillo did not invent Watergate, Oliver North, Albert Hakim, Richard Secord, or William Casey, who my father (a reasonable sort of guy) told me offhandedly at the Christmas dinner table, had most certainly been murdered by Reagan's operatives, with the consent of Casey himself. DeLillo has written this book, moreover, in the context of a contemporary fiction scene decisively shaped by the paranoid styles of Orwell, Burroughs, Mailer, Pynchon, and Didion. So *Libra*'s double narrative primes our desire for a paranoid finish to what the great naturalists always feared: that we lead lives arranged by and for the interests of others, that they are making history behind our backs. But unlike some of his predecessors in the paranoid novel (particularly Pynchon), DeLillo refuses to force a clinical reading of everyday life.

—Frank Lentricchia, "Libra as Postmodern Critique." *The South Atlantic Quarterly* 89, no. 2 (Spring 1990): pp. 438–441.

PAUL CIVELLO ON NICHOLAS BRANCH AS A PARODY OF EMILE ZOLA'S EXPERIMENTAL NOVELIST

[Paul Civello's essays have appeared in *Studies in American Fiction*, *The Hemingway Review*, and *Dictionary of Literary Biography*. In this excerpt, Civello shows how

Nicholas Branch functions as a contemporary parody of Emile Zola's experimental novelist.]

Zola, in comparing the novelist to a scientist, implicitly granted the novelist the same working assumptions of the classical scientist: that the universe was a conglomeration of discrete parts, that these parts interacted according to the laws of linear causality, that by studying these parts and the laws governing their behavior one could comprehend the universe, and, most importantly, that the scientist could stand apart from his experiment and watch it unfold objectively. In *Libra*, we see what amounts to a parody of Zola's experimental novelist in the character of Nicholas Branch. While Branch, in writing his history of the Kennedy assassination, is certainly not conducting an experiment, nor—he hopes—is he writing fiction, he nevertheless approaches his material and the task of assembling it into a cohesive narrative with the same assumptions that Zola's novelist had in mind. In other words, his interpretive paradigm is the same; however, the world in which he finds himself is far different, the material resisting such a paradigm. We first encounter Branch in a "small room," a metaphor that recurs throughout the novel. On its most fundamental level of meaning, the small room suggests isolation, and in Branch's context it initially seems to suggest an objective distance from the assassination he is trying to piece together. In this way, Branch is akin to the rational man of science, alone in his "book-filled room, the room of documents, the room of theories and dreams" (14). Yet such objectivity is immediately undercut when we learn that he is also in "the room of growing old" (14), his isolation granting him not perspective on the assassination but trapping him within the interpretive paradigm he brings to it. He cannot escape his paradigm, can never see the assassination in itself, and as a result can never construct a cohesive narrative that will render a "true" picture of the event. Branch and his facts, theories, and dreams grow old together. We learn that he has written very little since the CIA hired him to write the secret history of the assassination, that he cannot even reach the end of his accumulated data.

It is, of course, his paradigm which is primarily at fault, for it is based on a false conception of reality. Despite his growing frustration and despair, Branch continues to view his intractible data as an assembly of parts that can be linked, given enough rational analysis, into a cohesive pattern. "Everything is here" (181), we are told, in his room of theories and facts:

> Baptismal records, report cards, postcards, divorce petitions, canceled checks, daily timesheets, tax returns, property lists, postoperative x-rays, photos of knotted string, thousands of pages of testimony, of voices droning in hearing rooms in old courthouse buildings, an incredible haul of human utterance. (181)

This is but one list of several that are given in reference to Branch's data, the list itself indicative of the disjunctiveness of the parts as he perceives them. The implication is that while "everything" may be here, nothing is here, for reality is not composed of discrete parts, but of those parts *in relation* to one another. As Hayles has commented, in the field concept of reality, "The whole is composed of parts but cannot be reduced to them" (*Cosmic Web* 24). Branch wants such reductiveness, such simplicity. Yet only after years of study and frustration does Branch begin to see that simplicity is impossible. He begins to doubt that "the true nature of the event" (299) is contained in the various exhibits that the Curator sends him: "There is nothing to understand," he muses, "no insight to be had from these pictures and statistics" (299). Yet he remains at a loss as to an alternative paradigm.

In the course of the novel we begin to see that the various parts that comprise the Kennedy assassination are all connected in a non-linear, looping pattern of interconnecting systems. This systems pattern is the "true" relation of parts to one another, and therefore is the more accurate picture of the event itself. Branch, however, can only see fragments of this pattern due to his inherent limitations as a human being and to his interpretive paradigm which discounts those limitations. The looping pattern thus appears to him to be linear, and his *ex post facto* attempts to connect the parts into a cohesive whole are constrained by his imposition of the laws of linear causality. He wants to analyze the "six point nine seconds of heat and light" (15), as if the linear, chronological unfolding of events must contain the truth of the assassination. He searches in vain for a beginning, for an original cause of the assassination. Likewise, he searches in vain for an end—the linear paradigm, of course, positing a clearly defined beginning and end. In fact, Branch wonders "if he ought to despair of ever getting to the end" (59). "It is impossible," we are told, "to stop assembling data. The stuff keeps coming" (59). The assassination, just as it defied reduction to discrete parts, defies linear causality. Branch cannot bracket the event within a spatial or temporal frame. He cannot discern a linear pattern with a clear beginning and end. The pattern stretches beyond both space (i.e., Dallas) and time (i.e., six point nine seconds). The past is even "changing as he writes" (301).

Thus, rather than the accumulated data leading to greater knowledge, to greater certitude regarding the assassination, it leads to greater uncertainty. The more isolated facts Branch knows, the less he knows about the entire picture. "It is essential," he tells himself, "to master the data" (442), but it does him no good. The facts themselves are too ambiguous, their meaning too uncertain; moreover, they point in too many different directions, each direction resisting closure. As a result, Branch has no hope of coming to a definitive end to his investigation. In his frustration, he yearns for certitude, wanting "a thing to be what it is" (379); yet this wish goes unfulfilled. Toward the end of the novel he begins to accept uncertainty, abandoning his search for a linear pattern of cause and effect, and resigning himself to the indeterminate conclusion that "the conspiracy against the President was a rambling affair that succeeded in the short term due mainly to chance" (441).

—Paul Civello, "Undoing the Naturalistic Novel: Don Delillo's *Libra.*" *Arizona Quarterly* 48, no. 2 (Summer 1992): pp. 35–38.

HEINZ ICKSTADT ON THE THEATRICALIZATION OF EXPERIENCE

[Heinz Ickstadt is the coeditor of *The Thirties: Politics and Culture in a Time of Broken Dreams* (1987), American *Icons: Transatlantic Perspectives on Eighteenth-and Nineteenth-Century American Art* (1992), and *Faces of*

Fiction: Essays on American Literature and Culture from the Jacksonian Period to Postmodernity (2001). In this excerpt, Ickstadt explores places in the novel where the image invades and duplicates life.]

The book's title refers to Oswald's astrological sign (his birthday is October 18) and can be understood as a metaphor of his character (the scales whose balance can be easily disturbed) as well as of a narrated world that is precariously balanced between order and coincidence, yet ultimately ruled by chance. In such a fluid world all attempts at order and control are private fantasies seeking to become reality through plotting ("a world inside the world [...] a second existence, the private world floating out to three dimensions"). The novel not only consists of a network of such plots but operates at several levels of plotting. There is Oswald trying to convert the confusions of his life into a coherent plot; there is Everett who invents Oswald's identity as part of a larger plot; and there is Mackey, the anti-Castro veteran, who imposes his plot on Everett's. But the stories of these various plotters are in turn told by a narrator-figure whose plotting imagination despairingly tries to create sense and order out of a meaningless mass of information: Nicolas Branch, "retired senior analyst of the Central Intelligence Agency," a quasi-historian, and the novelist's alter-ego, is commissioned to write the "secret history" of the Kennedy-murder. His frustrations during fifteen years of research have their source not only in the quality of the data (even the "simple facts elude authentication"), but in the fact that "it is impossible to stop the data. The stuff keeps coming" (59). Because the past is thus "changing as he writes" (301), history will never be coherent or complete. Therefore, we may conclude, he can only write a tentative and "open" history, or rather, the fiction of a history that is DeLillo's novel.

Accordingly, there is an awareness in *Libra* that plotting and fiction-making are interrelated. Like Oswald, like Everett and Branch, the writer is locked in "his room of theories" or in fantasies of order to master an encroaching chaos of experience.[14] But whereas Oswald and the other conspirators desire to give meaning and purpose to their lives by imposing on it the shape of their fantasies, Branch/DeLillo hope to understand through their own fictions of coherence the meaning of these desires and designs. "Let's devote our lives"—thus Branch in one of the early chapters—"to understanding this moment, separating the elements of each crowded second. We will build theories that gleam like jade idols, intriguing systems of assumption, four-faced, graceful. We will follow the bullet trajectories backwards to the lives that occupy the shadows, actual men who moan in their dreams" (15). The "moaning" indicates the intensity of the desire and the desperate need for fictions of fulfillment. The world Oswald moves in is permeated with such fictions and fantasies, with dreams and wishes—a theatricalized world of images, of roles and role-play which Oswald duplicates in his own self-inventions and self-dramatizations and yet desires to escape from by entering the self-transcending world of history.[15]

As several critics have pointed out, there are three passages in particular where this peculiar quality of theatricalization (the invasion of everyday life by images and the extension and duplication of life through the image) becomes explicit. The first relates to Marina Oswald's first experience of being 'on camera':

> One evening they walked past a department store, just out strolling, and Marina looked at a television set in the window and saw the most remarkable thing, something so strange she had to stop and stare, grab hard at Lee. It was the world gone inside out. There they were gaping back at themselves from the TV screen. She was on television [...]. She walked out of the picture and then came back. She looked at Lee and June in the window, then turned to see them on the sidewalk. She kept looking from the window to the sidewalk. She kept walking out of the picture and coming back. She was amazed every time she saw herself return. (227)

The magic transformation Marina experiences—"the world gone inside out"—is the conversion of an imagined self into the heightened reality, the quasi-immanent transcendence of the publicly performing image of self. This sense that the relation between reality and fantasy has somehow been inverted, that the shared image of the real is more real than reality itself not only permeates the book but is a persistent motif in DeLillo's work from *Americana* to *Mao II*.[16] In *Libra*, the hatred some of the conspirators feel against Kennedy is not only connected with Cuba but with Kennedy's image-power: the power of his public image as well as his unlimited access to the world of images. "Bannister's rage toward the administration was partly a reaction to public life itself, to men who glow in the lens barrel of a camera. Kennedy magic, Kennedy charisma!" (62). When Kennedy arrives at the Dallas airport on the morning of November 22, he is experienced as "real" because he looks like his image ("he looked like himself, like photographs"), just as the crowd experiences its own reality from the knowledge that it participates in the shared dream of public image and event: "A contagion had brought them here, some mystery of common impulse, hundreds of thousands come from many histories and systems of being, come from some experience of the night before, a convergence of dreams, to stand together shouting as the Lincoln passed. They were here to be an event, a consciousness [...]" (393f.).

Although Oswald resents Marina's fascination with goods and images (which overlap in the glamorous image-world of advertising), his self-dramatization in the "Historical Diary" (where he wishfully projects and describes himself as a performer on the stage of history) as well as his posing, in several photographs, in the role of revolutionary make clear how deeply he is nevertheless part of the consumer culture that he despises. That is why DeLillo makes so much of Oswald's staring into the camera at the moment when he is shot: "He could see himself shot as the camera caught it. Through the pain he watched TV" (439). He knows that his death is "live," a televised "event." The self-transcendence he had been looking for in history, he finally achieves in this last knowledge of participation and belonging, of creating an image that can be—over and again—publicly consumed.[17]

NOTES

14. "Oswald becomes the strange semblance of the obsessed author-figure (he is called Nicolas Branch) who is ensconced in a room piled high with documents, who appears intermittently in *Libra* as DeLillo's double: Oswald, the double of a double, another man in his lonely writer's room who would tell the true tale of Dallas," Frank Lentricchia, *"Libra* as Postmodern Critique," 453; see also Eric Mottram, "The Real Needs of Man: Don DeLillo's Novels," *The New American Writing: Essays on American Literature Since 1970*, ed. Graham Clarke (London, 1990), 92f.

15. "His life had a single clear subject now, called Lee Harvey Oswald" (435). Lentricchia quite rightly points out the importance Oswald now gives to his full name. He accepts it (its weight and resonance) together with his role as man of history: Lee Harvey Oswald—John F. Kennedy.

16. Examples are accordingly numerous. In *The Names* (New York, 1989, 1982), 200, DeLillo has one of his protagonists (a film director) say: "Film is more than twentieth-century art. It's another part of the twentieth-century mind. It's the world seen from inside. We've come to a certain point in the history of film. If a thing can be filmed, film is implied in the thing itself. This is where we are. The twentieth century is on film. It's the filmed century. You have to ask yourself if there's anything about us more important than the fact that we're constantly on film, constantly watching ourselves [...]."

17. DeLillo strongly emphasizes this aspect of ritualistic participation, of the community's unconscious life played out in the fate of the protagonist, as is especially noticeable in the reflections of the wife of one of the conspirators' who watches the event "live" and then in endless replay: "There was something in Oswald's face, a glance at the camera before he was shot, that put him here in the audience, among the rest of us, sleepless in our homes—a glance, a way of telling us that he knows who we are and how we feel, that he has brought our perceptions and interpretations into his sense of the crime. [...] He is commenting on the documentary footage even as it is being shot. Then he himself is shot, and shot, and shot, and the look becomes another kind of knowledge. But he has made us part of his dying" (447).

> —Heinz Ickstadt, "Loose Ends and Patterns of Coincidence in Don DeLillo's *Libra.*" *Historiographic Metafiction in Modern American and Canadian Literature*, ed. Bernd Engler and Kurt Muller, (Paderborn, Germany: Ferdinand Schoningh, 1994): pp. 305–308.

John Johnston on the Invention of Oswald

[John Johnston is the author of *Carnival of Repetition: Gaddis' The Recognitions and Postmodern Theory* (1990) and *Information Multiplicity: American Fiction in the Age of Media Saturation* (1998). In this excerpt, Johnston discusses the creation of Oswald as an example of the complex relationship between fiction and reality.]

The central ambiguity of Oswald's identity is framed by and resonates through the entire series of men in small rooms who echo and repeat each other throughout the novel. Again, it is Win Everett who initiates the series when he begins the process of inventing "Oswald." Not only doubling Oswald's own efforts to fabricate alternate identities, Everett's invention is also self-referential and metafictional. "Stalking a victim," he reflects, "can be a way of organizing one's loneliness, making a network out of it, a fabric of connections. Desperate men give their solitude a purpose and a destiny" (141). Presumably referring to his own invention of one such desperate man, Kennedy's future assassin, Everett's reflections also apply to himself. Leading a life of quiet desperation (Thoreau's phrase reverberates through the novel), he organizes a conspiracy that gradually becomes his own purpose or "destiny" as an alternative to the banal details of teaching at a small town college and the daily rituals of domestic life. His sense that "some things we wait for all our lives without knowing it" (27), as he says to his fellow conspirators, clearly echoes Oswald's feeling that his (Oswald's) life was leading toward a momentous event in which he would finally realize his historic destiny. For Oswald, this fulfillment means breaking free of the series of small rooms that has hitherto defined his life's trajectory. Ironically, Nicholas Branch reflects upon—but also becomes part of—the series when he acknowledges that "it has taken him all these years to learn that his subject is not politics or violent crime but men in small rooms. Is he one of them now? Frustrated, stuck, self-watching, looking for a means of connection" (181). And finally, appending his "Author's Note," DeLillo literally inscribes himself as the series' last frame.

Everett, Oswald, Branch, and by extension DeLillo the author thus form a series of men in small rooms who are both aligned and differentiated through a series of variously embedded assumptions about the difference between fiction and reality. At the center of this complex of relationships is "Oswald" himself. And what is most interesting about "Oswald" is the fact that he was not simply an actual historical personage around whom DeLillo constructed a quasi-documentary fiction, but in a very critical sense a fiction already created by various intelligence agencies and police networks, then refined and amplified by the Warren Commission and mass media—all, to be sure, with different motives and "design" criteria. In the *Rolling Stone* article cited earlier, DeLillo comments on this remarkable fact:

"Lee Harvey Oswald" often seems a secret design worked out by men who will never surface—a procedural diagram, a course in fabricated biography. Who put him together? He is not an actor so much as he is a character, a fictional character who first emerges as such in the year 1957.... Oswald seemed scripted out of doctored photos, tourist cards, change-of-address cards, mail-order forms, visa applications, altered signatures, pseudonyms. (24)

But equally remarkable is the extent to which Oswald himself, perhaps unwittingly, has participated in his own fabrication, for the historical evidence reveals that there was not only this fictitious, "scripted" Oswald but also a plurality of alter egos and "fake" identities disseminated by the (or a?) Lee Harvey Oswald, who seems to have employed an astonishing range of names and variants for purposes of identification or whenever a signature was required. All of which leads DeLillo to hazard that "Oswald was his own double" (24). But which Oswald was whose double? Indeed, in this convergence of conspiratorial fabrication and schizophrenic dispersion, human identity is so radically uncertain that the very notion of a "double" now seems faintly anachronistic if not actually obsolete. In any event, the world of espionage in which Oswald operated was such a dizzying labyrinth of reflecting and refracting surfaces that it is quite possible, as DeLillo himself speculates, that Oswald might have worked for one intelligence agency while appearing to work for another, yet never really knowing which was which.

—John Johnston, "Superlinear Fiction or Historical Diagram: Don DeLillo's *Libra*." *Modern Fiction Studies* 40, no. 2 (Summer 1994): pp. 330–332.

GLEN THOMAS ON THE FRAGMENTARY NATURE OF HISTORY

[Glen Thomas has published articles on Don DeLillo, Miles Franklin, and Patrick White. In this excerpt, Thomas discusses the novel as an argument that history is essentially a product of fragmentary perceptions.]

Don DeLillo's first novel concludes with the narrator retracing the route of the 1963 Presidential motorcade through the streets of Dallas and on to the hospital where John F. Kennedy was declared dead. DeLillo again retraces this route in his 1988 novel *Libra*, a text that offers a threefold narrative structure: a "biography" of Lee Harvey Oswald; a plot to make an attempt on the life of President Kennedy, which is designed to be a "spectacular miss" (*Libra* 51); and the efforts of the retired secret service agent Nicholas Branch, who is trying to write a secret history of the assassination for the CIA. The novel thus melds historical fact (the events in Dallas in 1963) and fiction (the details of the plot to scare the President into attacking Cuba). Further complicating this structure is the wealth of other texts that surround the assassination itself, all of which strive for the status of being accepted as a factual account of "what really happened." To date, no one account of the Kennedy assassination has achieved definitive status: Gerald Posner estimates that by 1992 over 2,000 books had been written about the assassination (ix). *Libra* is therefore one more text in this continually proliferating chain of texts surrounding an event characterized by indeterminacy and dispute.

Barbie Zelitzer argues that the assassination narrative is characterized by an "absence of closure" (105). Since the publication of the Warren Commission Report in 1964, the official account of Kennedy's death has been regarded with suspicion. Within months of the publication of the 26-volume report, articles critical of its findings began appearing in mainstream media outlets such as *Esquire* and the *New Republic*: "[By] the end of the decade, the critics had aired conspiracy theories involving pro-Castro and anti-Castro proponents; the Dallas police; the CIA, FBI, and Secret Service; organized crime; Texas right-wingers; and oil magnates" (Zelitzer 107). It may be argued then that a number of oppositional histories quickly arose in response to the official version. Subsequent events in American political history, most notably the Watergate scandal, prompted an increased distrust of official explanations. By the end of the 1970s, public doubt over the findings of the Warren Commission persuaded Congress to reopen the assassination in the form of the House Select Committee on Assassinations (Zelitzer 117). The major finding of this committee was that President Kennedy's death was the result of a conspiracy, although no names or organizations were offered as the culprits. The revaluations of the assassination continued throughout the 1980s and culminated (to date, at least) in the 1991 release of Oliver Stone's *JFK*. Stone claimed to be "acting as historian in retelling the story of Kennedy's death" (Zelitzer 202), a statement that complicates the boundaries between conventional demarcations of fact and fiction. In Stone's film, as in *Libra*, the distinction between the two categories is disrupted, so that the historical record becomes another form of fiction (which resulted, in part, in both DeLillo and Stone being accused of distortion, bias, and plain lies in their respective representations of the Kennedy assassination).

Libra asserts that Oswald did not act alone and that there was a conspiracy. The novel may be read in the light of textualist theories of history, in that *Libra* refuses to see the historical record as a fixed or stable entity but instead as the product of interpretation. Hayden White argues that history is always and nothing more than a narrative construction: "Confronted with a chaos of 'facts' the historian must choose, sever and carve them up for narrative purposes" (*Tropics* 55). Traditional forms of history find their coherence in narrative structure, a chronological form with a beginning, middle, and end, unencumbered by questions regarding the suitability of such a form (see White, *Content* 31, for a discussion of those who simply "practice" history). *Libra* challenges this historical form by suggesting that random actions and the workings of chance will connect and collide with each other in a way that cannot be anticipated or adequately explained, in what is almost a chaos theory of history. It is this randomness that prevents Nicholas Branch from actually writing his projected history, as from his perspective there is no orderly pattern of events that culminated in the assassination. Instead, as will be discussed, the information available refuses to coalesce and remains stubbornly fragmentary.

—Glen Thomas, "History, Biography, and Narrative in Don DeLillo's *Libra*." *Twentieth Century Literature* 43, no. 1 (Spring 1997): pp. 107–109.

SKIP WILLMAN ON OSWALD'S ALIENATION IN A CONSUMER CULTURE

[Skip Willman's essays have appeared in *Modern Fiction Studies* and *Contemporary Literature*. In this excerpt, Willman considers the roots of Oswald's social alienation in the novel.]

In a provocative formulation of the impact of American society on Lee Harvey Oswald, DeLillo remarks, "His life in small rooms is the antithesis of the life America seems to promise its citizens: the life of consumer fulfillment" ("'Outsider'" 52). He adds that the amazement of Oswald's wife at the "world of American consumer promise ... must have caused an enormous tension in his life" (52). Since Oswald was "barely employable" (DeLillo, "Art" 303), he was unable to provide Marina with the means to participate in this "consumer promise." DeLillo speculates further on the relationship between consumer society and contemporary violence:

> I see contemporary violence as a kind of sardonic response to the promise of consumer fulfillment in America. Again we come back to these men in small rooms who can't get out and who have to organize their desperation and their loneliness, who have to give it a destiny and who often end up doing this through violent means. I see this desperation against the backdrop of brightly colored packages and products and consumer happiness and every promise that American life makes day by day and minute by minute everywhere we go. ("'Outsider'" 57–58)

According to DeLillo, late capitalism offers a fantasy bribe in the promise of consumer fulfillment to offset its necessary product: social fragmentation and atomization. In *Libra*, Oswald's remarks betray a cynical awareness of this arrangement within late capitalism: "He would start saving right away for a washing machine and a car. They'd get an apartment with a balcony, their own furniture for a change, modern pieces, sleek and clean. These are standard ways to stop being lonely" (317). However, the lived experience of "men in small rooms" divorced from the social totality and the stream of history sets the stage for the "sardonic response" of contemporary violence.

DeLillo's description of Oswald's "alienation" demonstrates the effects of what Jameson calls "reification": "the way in which, under capitalism, the older traditional forms of human activity are instrumentally reorganized and 'taylorized,' analytically fragmented and reconstructed according to various rational models of efficiency, and essentially restructured along the lines of a differentiation between means and ends" (*Signatures* 10). More importantly for our analysis of Oswald, Jameson suggests that reification has a damaging effect upon the individual subject because it is "a process that affects our cognitive relationship with the social totality. It is a disease of that mapping function whereby the individual subject projects and models his or her insertion into the collectivity" ("Reflections" 146). Throughout the novel, Oswald laments his inability to find his own niche in society: "He feels he is living at the center of an emptiness. He wants to sense a structure that includes him, a definition clear enough to specify where he belongs. But the system floats right through him, through everything, even the revolution. He is a zero in the system" (357). Translating this dilemma into Jameson's terms, Oswald's fundamental problem involves the failure of ideology to provide him with an adequate cognitive map of the social totality, a problem exacerbated by his inability to participate in the compensations offered by the "fantasy bribe" of consumerism.

> —Skip Willman, "Traversing the Fantasies of the JFK Assassination: Conspiracy and Contingency in Don DeLillo's *Libra.*" *Contemporary Literature* 39, no. 3 (Fall 1998): pp. 421–422.

DAVID T. COURTWRIGHT ON DELILLO AS NOMOTHETIC HISTORIAN

[David T. Courtwright is Distinguished Professor of History at the University of North Florida and the author of several books on American social history, including *Violent Land: Single Men and Social Disorder from the Frontier to the Inner City* (1996) and *Forces of Habit: Drugs and the Making of the Modern World* (2001). In this excerpt, Courtwright considers DeLillo's portrayal of Oswald a piece of "nomothetic" history, that is, a representation of a man whose life is subject to the larger forces that direct human affairs.]

DeLillo has never claimed that *Libra* is an argument for what really happened, only an exploration of one plausible variation.

There's no point getting too preoccupied with "the endless fact-rubble of the investigation," as the CIA historian Nicholas Branch, another DeLillo invention, puts it. Still, I found myself thinking hard about the significance of Oswald's last miss. It compels reflection, and not simply because of the forensic puzzle. I now believe that, whatever DeLillo lost in historical credibility by having Oswald miss, he gained in thematic coherence. The third shot, in its own way, exemplifies the art-actuality tension at the heart of historical fiction.

When historians answer the how and why questions of human behavior, their explanations generally fall into one of two camps. We call these, if you'll excuse a bit of philosophical jargon, the nomothetic and idiographic. Nomothetic writers explain things in lawlike terms, identifying the forces that govern human affairs and incorporating them into their explanation sketches. A student of revolution, for example, might appeal to the axiom that, when the price of bread rises, discontent rises with it. Nomothetic historians subordinate the individual to powerful physical, biological, economic, social, and psychological forces that they believe are the keys to understanding the human past.

Idiographic historians try to understand unique and nonrecurring events by focusing on particular historical actors and empathically reconstructing the choices confronting them at a given moment in time. Their subjects operate under various constraints and pressures. But they—some of them, anyway—are able to use reason to evaluate possible responses and will to carry through. It is these free individual decisions, some good and some bad, that propel history. The slaves were freed, not because Northern industrialism was destined to triumph over Southern slavery through some abstract dialectical process, but because Lincoln understood their emancipation to be both morally correct and strategically advantageous. Idiographic history permits, though it does not require, heroic actions. Nomothetic history, being deterministic, precludes them. (...)

DeLillo is a writer who began with a nomothetic (or, perhaps, considering the occult flavoring, pseudo-nomothetic) approach. He stuck to it, refining it in his breakthrough work of the 1980s, and kept it prominently on display in *Mao II* (1991) and

Underworld (1997). His characters are caught, not in the linear, cause-and-effect determinism of classical naturalism, but a looping pattern of interconnected systems. They try, not always successfully, to name those systems, understand them, escape them, or just survive them from day to day. Jack Gladney, the historian-everyman of *White Noise* (1985), wakes up in the small hours, paralyzed by his own racking fears, lacking even the will and strength to get out of bed. Eventually, he has to cope with a real nightmare, an "airborne toxic event" packing a dozen poisons, moving across the land "like some death ship in a Norse legend." In *Mao II* and *Underworld*, the characters continually voice their anxieties, their sense of subjection to something that is big, sinister, Out There. "The future belongs to crowds," we're told in *Mao II*, a novel in which the archindividualist winds up dead. "What do we know?" a character asks in *Underworld*. "That everything's connected," answers another. DeLillo's prose sometimes takes on an overtly sociological character. "Capital burns off the nuance in a culture," he observes in the epilogue to *Underworld*. That's a sentence Max Weber might have written on a good day.

In *Libra*, Oswald becomes Lee Oswald, loser, through an unhappy combination of inborn traits and social circumstances. Like almost everyone who has studied him, DeLillo was struck by the disparity between Oswald's taped debates on Cuba—articulate performances by someone of obvious intelligence—and his childlike writing and difficulty in reading. Dyslexia frustrates Oswald, holds him back from scholastic accomplishment and upward movement into a middle-class career. A successful paper-pusher would not have shot at the president. The boy is poor and fatherless in the bargain. His natural father died before his birth. In 1945 Marguerite married an older man, an engineer named Edwin Ekdahl, but they divorced acrimoniously in 1948. From that point on, the "basic Oswald memory" was sharing a series of cramped spaces with his mother.

—David T. Courtwright, "Why Oswald Missed: Don DeLillo's *Libra*." *Novel History: Historians and Novelists Confront America's Past (and Each Other)*, ed. Mark C. Carnes, (New York: Simon and Schuster, 2001): pp. 86–87, 87–88, 89.

[Stuart Hutchinson is the author of *Henry James—An
American as Modernist* (1982) and *The American Scene:
Essays on Nineteenth-Century American Literature* (1991).
He is also the editor of critical volumes on Henry James,
George Eliot, and Mark Twain. In this excerpt,
Hutchinson explores the ways in which characters who
live in isolation, such as Oswald, Win Everett, and David
Ferrie, sustain themselves with the idea that they possess
secret knowledge.]

Realising the course of daily life, *Libra* reveals the way men
release their 'quiet desperation' in violent activity, thereby
seeking to fend off the disintegration of 'finding themselves
alone in small rooms'. In a reflection on this motif in his work,
DeLillo has said of Oswald: 'His life in small rooms is the
antithesis of the life America seems to promise its citizens: the
life of consumer fulfilment' (DeCurtis, p. 290). Thoreau had
already lived this antithesis, but with positive effect, in his small
room at Walden, where he revealed ultimate harmonies between
the self and the world. Oswald and other characters in *Libra*,
however, experience life in small rooms as deprivation. It leads to
attempts at fulfilment Thoreau would regard as contrary to
nature, even though they echo his own desire for harmony, as we
see in Oswald's Marxist political gesture which is the epigraph to
Part I of the novel: 'Happiness is taking part in the struggle,
where there is no borderline between one's personal world, and
the world in general.' Oswald's eventual experience in the USSR
will fall far short of this happiness, but when we first meet him
he is living with his mother in a basement in the Bronx, a district
DeLillo, with a naturalist's understanding of the contribution of
environment to character, records with personal authority:
'Oswald and I lived within six or seven blocks of each other in the
Bronx' (DeCurtis, p. 287). From this small room Oswald escapes
to ride 'the subway to the ends of the city, two hundred miles of
track' (p. 3). Confined spaces can be burial alive, but an
underground world can also seem a secret arena of power:

There is a world inside the world.
He rode the subway up to Inwood, out to Sheepshead Bay.
There were serious men down there, rocking in the copper
light. He saw chinamen, beggars, men who talked to God,
men who lived on the trains ... He rode between cars, gripping
the heavy chain. He felt the friction of the ride in his teeth....
He liked feeling they were on the edge.... The wheels touched
off showers of blue-white sparks, tremendous hissing bursts,
on the edge of no-control.... He was riding just to ride. The
noise had a power and a human force. The dark had a power.
He stood at the front of the first car, hands flat against the
glass. The view down the tracks was a form of power.... The
noise was pitched to a fury he located in the mind, a satisfying
wave of rage and pain.
Never again in his short life, never in the world, would he
feel this inner power, rising to a shriek, this secret force of the
soul, in the tunnels under New York. (p. 13)

Along with the other men presumed to be serious and talking to
God, Oswald in the subway shares the exaltation of Win Everett,
who from the small rooms of his exile by the CIA at 'Texas
Woman's University' (p. 19) begets the plot to fire a shot,
intended to miss, at JFK. According to Win the plan to stage an
'electrifying event' (p. 27), so as to implicate Castro and arouse
the US to repossess Cuba, 'speaks to something deep inside me.
It has a powerful logic. I've felt it unfolding for weeks, like a
dream whose meaning slowly becomes apparent. This is the
condition we've always wanted to reach. It's the life insight, the
life secret, and we have to extend it, guard it carefully' (p. 28).
Numerous DeLillo characters relish the seeming potency of
secret knowledge which, by seeming to place them at the pitch
and limit of things, 'the edge of no-control', nourishes the self-
aggrandisement and metaphysical intimations their deprivation
yearns for. If Oswald's life in *Libra* is to be regarded as tragic, it
is the tragedy of a human being who is never able or enabled to
feel more empowered than in experiencing in the fury of the
subway a correlative to, and release from, his own 'rage and pain'.
DeLillo himself, in his sympathy for Oswald, seems to recognise
this tragedy, but in the above passage he also participates in
Oswald's sense of exaltation in the subway, as if he himself

actually were a latter-day Whitman able to experience the 'force of the soul' (whatever this term can mean in the late twentieth century) in America's powerful self-manifestations. DeLillo endorses the concept that the course of history is absolute in referring in interview to the epigraph to Part I of the novel (DeCurtis, p. 290), and in the novel itself when he has the epigraph echoed in Oswald's consciousness: 'He thought the only end to isolation was to reach the point where he was no longer separated from the true struggles that went on around him. The name we give to this point is history' (p. 248). 'We' clearly associates the author with this flatulent pronouncement about history, even though (in a novel published in 1988) he has already exhibited Oswald's mid-century delusion in believing the 'dynamics of history favor the Soviet Union' (p. 113). Later, David Ferrie is also to regard history as an absolute force, while seeing it as an energy an individual can transcend. Announcing a theory that can be neither proved nor disproved, Ferrie tells Oswald: 'There's no such thing as coincidence.' He continues:

> We didn't arrange your job in that building or set up the motorcade route. We don't have that kind of reach or power. There's something else that's generating this event. A pattern outside experience. Something that *jerks* you out of the spin of history. I think you've had it backwards all this time. You want-ed to enter history. Wrong approach ... What you really want is out. Get out. Jump out. Find your place and name on anoth-er level. (p. 384)

Yet Ferrie, in DeLillo's and Oswald's words, is 'strange even to himself', his take on life understandably skewed by his 'rare and horrific condition that had no cure. His body was one hundred percent bald' (p. 29). He is one of DeLillo's displayed paranoiacs, his other definition of history being entirely conspiratorial: 'It's the sum total of all the things they aren't telling us' (p. 321). He longs for the ultimate reality of the Bomb so that he can retreat into the imagined gratification of his version of a small room, a shelter 'deep in the ground, isolated, with food and water for many months.... How satisfying he thought to live in a hole ... just to eke out extra time while all hell thundered on the surface' (p. 29). There, like Oswald riding the subway, he can feel in

harmony (in that he would be immune) with history as enormous force. Like Win with his plot, he can feel authorial and authentic, indulging in a version of the Joycean 'silence, exile and cunning' DeLillo himself, in a throwaway remark, has spoken of adopting.[10]

NOTES

10. Thomas LeClair, 'An Interview with Don DeLillo', *Contemporary Literature*, 23 (1983) pp. 19–31: 20.

—Stuart Hutchinson, "DeLillo's Libra and the Real." *The Cambridge Quarterly* 30, no. 2 (2001): pp. 122–124.

White Noise

White Noise offers a humorous representation of the postmodern American family—a family practically lost in the flurry of media images, consumerist messages, and the toxic waste products of a high-technology culture. For Jack Gladney, the fantasy of consumer contentment ultimately fails to cover the deep paranoia about death that underlies his everyday life. DeLillo's narrative gradually reveals the grandeur and the ludicrousness of postmodern anxiety as his protagonist's discomfort ascends to a murderous rage, only to conclude with a botched murder attempt, a toxic sunset, and a renewed reverence for the supermarket.

Part One, entitled "Waves and Radiation" begins as Jack Gladney, Chairman of the Department of Hitler Studies at College-on-the-Hill, observes Fall move-in day at the student dormitories. He returns home to his wife, Babette, who is an adult education teacher and a volunteer reader for the blind. Both Jack and Babette have an assortment of children from various previous marriages. Babette has two sons by a former husband who lives in Western Australia, a toddler named Wilder who is in her custody and an eight-year-old named Eugene who lives with his father. She also has a grade school age daughter named Denise by a former husband named Bob Pardee. Jack has a grade school-age daughter named Steffie by his first and fourth wife, Dana Breedlove, a fourteen year-old son named Heinrich by his second wife Janet Savory, and a twelve year-old daughter named Bee, who lives with his third wife Tweedy Browner.

Jack's claim to fame in academia is the Department of Hitler Studies at College-on-the-Hill, which he established. Hitler scholars must at some point nod to Jack as an authority. Jack is somewhat friendly with professors from the popular culture department of the college, known as "American environments," but Murray Jay Siskind, a visiting lecturer on living icons, becomes his fast friend over lunch. Murray, who wants to do with Elvis what Jack did with Hitler, asks for Jack's advice; he also gives Jack a referral for a German tutor named Howard Dunlop so Jack can learn German in time for the upcoming Hitler conference at the college.

Denise and Steffie's school is being inspected for toxic poisoning due to the fact that a few students and a teacher have displayed unusual symptoms; therefore the two girls are home from school.

Jack and Babette run into Murray at the supermarket on a regular basis, where he fawns over Babette and theorizes about the supermarket as a repository of cultural significance. Two weeks later, when he has Babette and Jack over for dinner at his boarding house, he calls television "waves and radiation;" it is a primal force and a keeper of sacred formulas that only the keenest observer can experience.

On the way home from dinner, Babette tells Jack she is having memory problems. Denise's alcoholic gambling father, Bob Pardee, comes over to visit and takes the kids out to dinner, while Jack drives Babette to read the tabloids to Mr. Treadwell, an elderly blind man. Treadwell is nowhere to be found. Later he and his elderly sister are found alive but shaken, having gotten lost for four days and nights in the Mid-Village Mall.

Denise tells Jack she found a prescription bottle of Dylar in Babette's things and is worried. Jack meets Tweedy Browner at the airport, who flies in from Washington just ahead of Bee, their daughter. While they wait for Bee's flight to arrive, they watch shaken passengers disembark from a flight whose plane's engines died for some time, dropping them four miles before they turned back on. Bee arrives, and Jack takes her to his home for Christmas.

Part Two, entitled "The Airborne Toxic Event," begins as Heinrich, on the roof with his binoculars, spots a dark cloud of smoke in the distance. A tank car has derailed outside of town, and a toxic cloud of Nyodene Derivative, a by-product of insecticide, is leaking out. On the radio, announcers call it an "airborne toxic event," and officials on loudspeakers order residents to evacuate. Jack's family is directed to a boy scout camp, where a group called "simuvac," short for "simulated evacuation," checks people in with computers. In an absurd twist of logic, "simuvac" is using this real event to practice their simulations. When Jack tells the official that he stepped out of his car to pump gas while the toxic cloud was overhead, the official enters this information into his computer, which happens to hold a file on Jack's complete health history. The computer concludes that Jack's health is greatly endangered.

Part Three is called "Dylarama." Murray will win the Elvis chair, due to the death of a colleague who had preeminence. Since the toxic event, men walk around in mylar suits with German shepherds measuring toxicity, sunsets are more vivid and blazing than ever before, and the experience of *déjà vu* has become a widespread problem. Jack finds a bottle of Dylar taped to the underside of the radiator. Since Babette has previously denied taking any medication, Jack calls her doctor, who denies ever prescribing it and has never heard of Dylar. Jack then takes a pill to Winnie Richards, a research neurochemist on campus, who determines that it is some kind of psychopharmaceutical. He confronts Babette about it, and she tells him she obtained the pill by participating in a drug trial advertised in the tabloids. She had to sleep with the project manager in order to obtain them, and the condition she was trying to medicate was her overwhelming fear of death. The medication has not worked. Jack admits to his own fear of death, revealing to her that he was exposed to Nyodene Derivative and was given a virtual death sentence by the "simuvac" computer.

Jack tells Denise that Babette was taking the Dylar to help her memory loss. Denise does not believe him and refuses to give the pills back. Steffie's mother, Dana Breedlove, a CIA agent, writes asking her to pay a visit to her in Mexico City. Jack confronts Babette in the middle of the night asking for the name of the drug researcher; he wants to try the drug himself. Babette refuses. He then finds Winnie Richards and asks her to find out who makes the drug. Winnie tells him to forget about the drug and confront his fear.

The town's insane asylum burns down one day, and Jack and Heinrich stand across the street to watch. Suddenly an acrid smell of burning synthetic material permeates the air, which drives the observers away.

Jack is now hopelessly preoccupied with his own death. One morning he sees a white-haired man sitting in a chair in the backyard and hides in the bathroom, thinking it is Death. It is Vernon Dickey, Babette's father, paying a surprise visit. Before

Vernon leaves, he gives Jack his German-made Zumwalt automatic gun. Jack searches through the trash compactor for Babette's remaining pills, eager to calm his fears.

Ninety Hitler scholars arrive at the college for a conference. Jack gives a five-minute welcome in disjointed German, then hides in his office for most of the time. On the advice of his doctor, Jack goes to the neighboring Glassboro for medical tests, where the doctor tells him the Nyodene Derivative in his system may lead to a nebulous mass. Jack takes a long walk with Murray, who tells him that people will depend on him to be brave in the face of death. He suggests to Jack that one is either a killer or a doer in this world, and when a killer kills, he gains life-credit. Jack starts carrying the Zumwalt automatic with him everywhere.

Winnie Richards reads an article about the Dylar project in one of her journals and tells Jack about it. Apparently the project manager, Willie Mink, was kicked off the trial because there was a controversy surrounding him and a motel room in Iron City, where a woman with a ski mask was seen to enter on a regular basis. Jack recognizes the description of his wife and is irate. He steals his neighbors' car, drives to the Roadway Motel in Iron City, finds Wink's room, and walks in to find Wink delusional, popping the Dylar pills like candy. After some conversation, Jack shoots Wink twice in the stomach and puts the gun in Mink's hand so it appears to be a suicide. Mink shoots Jack in the wrist, Jack tells a foggy Mink that the gun was in his hand the whole time, and then drives them both to a nearby clinic run by atheistic nuns. Jack drives home, leaving the bloody car in the neighbors' driveway.

Jack and his family sit on an overpass watching the brilliant sunset with the other local residents, an activity that has become quite regular. Jack no longer returns calls from his doctor. As the novel ends, Jack reflects on the fact that the supermarket shelves have been rearranged. People are confused and move in disjointed patterns. He has taken up Murray's reverence for the supermarket, saying "this is the language of waves and radiation, or how the dead speak to the living."

LIST OF CHARACTERS IN

White Noise

Jack Gladney is the Chairman of the Hitler Studies Department at College-on-the-Hill in a town called Blacksmith. He has an intense fear of his own death, which leads him to lie to his doctors about being exposed to toxic chemicals. He begins carrying a gun, and kills a drug researcher named Willie Mink in an attempt to avenge his wife's infidelity and stave off his own death.

Babette is Jack's fifth wife and the mother of Wilder and Denise. She is secretly terrified of her own death, and sleeps with Willie Mink in exchange for an experimental drug called Dylar, which supposedly treats that fear. She hides this affair and her use of the drug, but eventually her daughter Denise finds the prescription bottle, leading to Jack's confronting Babette and learning the truth.

Murray Jay Siskind is a visiting lecturer on living icons for the popular culture department of College-on-the-Hill and a New York émigré. He aspires to create a department of Elvis studies at the college and eventually gets his wish. He becomes a close friend to Jack, influencing him with his somewhat quirky perspectives on life and cultural data. When comforting Jack about his fatal exposure to toxic chemicals, Murray suggests to Jack that killers gain life-credit every time they take a life, which influences Jack to shoot Willie Mink.

Heinrich is Jack's son by his second wife, Janet Savory. At age fourteen, he is already an intellectual and a skeptic. Normally a pessimist and a loner, he blooms as an entertainer and lecturer when he begins sharing his knowledge to a group of interested listeners during the evacuation at the Boy Scout Camp.

Denise is Babette's grade school-age daughter by a former husband named Bob Pardee. She finds Babette's prescription bottle of Dylar and is unsettled by it, pressuring Jack to investigate whether her mother is a drug addict. When she does not get straight answers from Jack, she refuses to surrender the pills and eventually throws them away.

Steffie is Jack's grade school-age daughter by his first and fourth wife, Dana Breedlove. Steffie has a knack for sympathizing acutely with people she sees on television. She visits her mother, a CIA agent, in Mexico City, returning with stories of Dana's tireless work: reading novels for embedded codes or messages.

Wilder is Babette's toddler son from a former marriage to a man who now lives in Western Australia. Wilder seems to possess a deep and unexplainable power, crying for almost seven hours straight and riding his tricycle across the expressway unscathed.

Mr. Treadwell is an old blind man that Babette reads the tabloids to on a regular basis as part of her volunteer work. He and his elderly sister disappear and are found four days later having been stranded in Mid-Village Mall, taking shelter in an abandoned cookie shack.

Winnie Richards is a psychobiologist and a research neurochemist at College-on-the-Hill. She analyzes one of Babette's Dylar pills as a favor to Jack, finding it to be an unknown psychopharmaceutical. After reading a story in one of her psychobiology journals about the Dylar project, she informs Jack as to the whereabouts of the project's former director, Willie Mink. Jack uses this information to confront Willie and shoot him.

Vernon Dickey is Babette's father and Jack's father-in-law. During his visit with Babette and the family, Vernon takes Jack aside secretly and gives him his gun—a Zumwalt automatic. Though Jack refuses the gun, Vernon convinces him to keep it. This is the gun Jack uses to shoot Willie Mink.

Willie Mink/Mr. Gray is the project director for a research trial for an anti-fear drug called Dylar. He agrees to give a desperate Babette the medication, accepting sex as compensation. Jack tracks him down and shoots him twice in the stomach, after which Mink shoots Jack in the wrist and becomes unconscious. Jack resuscitates him and takes him to a clinic.

Tweedy Browner is one of Jack's former wives and Bee's mother. She's unhappily married to her government agent-husband, Malcolm.

Bee is Jack's daughter with Tweedy Browner. When she visits at Christmas, her sophistication makes the family feel self-conscious.

Janet Savory is Heinrich's mother, Janet has moved to a secluded Hindu community called an ashram—she wants Heinrich to visit her.

Bob Pardee, Denise's father, is a businessman who works for the government.

CRITICAL VIEWS ON
White Noise

MICHAEL W. MESSMER ON THE BLURRING OF THE REAL AND THE FAKE

[Michael W. Messmer is an Associate Professor of History at Virginia Commonwealth University. In this excerpt, Messmer explores the novel's "hyperreality" through the theories of Jean Baudrillard and Umberto Eco.]

What I think Baudrillard's and Eco's work reveals is a complex blurring of the "real" and the "fake," of the "real" and the "simulation" in all aspects of postmodern life, in the culture of the simulacrum, in nuclear culture, in the "America of furious hyperreality." A brilliant evocation of that blurring occurs in Don DeLillo's recent novel *White Noise* and a brief scrutiny of it can help to bring the discussion thus far into concrete focus. DeLillo is one of the most acute and penetrating observers of American hyperreality, not least because of the mordant humor he brings to his dissections of the fads and foibles of this society of the spectacle in which we find ourselves embedded.[10]

One of the central events in *White Noise* is a major spillage of a highly toxic chemical which then forms an immense, drifting black cloud of lethality (the "Airborne Toxic Event") and forces the evacuation of a small college town, including the history professor who is the book's main character and his family. They become the *subjects* of a disaster (one which uncannily anticipated the Bhopal disaster in India), thus reversing the position they (and we) normally assume of being *observers* of disaster. One of this family's rituals is to watch television together every Friday night:

> That night, a Friday, we gathered in front of the set, as was the custom and the rule, with take-out Chinese. There were floods, earthquakes, mud slides, erupting volcanoes. We'd never before been so attentive to our duty, our Friday assembly. Heinrich was not sullen, I was not bored. Steffie, brought

close to tears by a sitcom husband arguing with his wife, appeared totally absorbed in these documentary clips of calamity and death. Babette tried to switch to a comedy about a group of racially mixed kids who build their own communication satellite. She was startled by the force of our objection. We were otherwise silent, watching houses slide into the ocean, whole villages crackle and ignite in a mass of advancing lava. Every disaster made us wish for more, for something bigger, grander, more sweeping. (64)

For DeLillo's imagined scenario, substitute another. Suppose that nuclear weapons were used in one of the current wars raging across the globe, perhaps in the Iran–Iraq war, and that the explosions were filmed for television news (as no doubt they would be). Does not DeLillo's text capture one aspect of what the millions and millions of evening news watchers would feel? Does it not capture a sense of what the tens of millions of viewers of actual nuclear explosions have felt?

The professor in *White Noise* wonders why, why did and his family enjoy watching these disasters? For an answer he consults the popular culture experts among his fellow faculty members in the Department of American Environments. "Why is it," he asks, "that decent, well-meaning and responsible people find themselves intrigued by catastrophe when they see it on television?" In answering him, one of the pop culture specialists graphically evokes an important aspect of the culture of simulacra and hyperreality:

"The flow is constant," Alfonse said. "Words, pictures, numbers, facts, graphics, statistics, specks, waves, particles, motes. Only a catastrophe gets our attention. We want them, we need them, we depend on them. As long as they happen somewhere else. This is where California comes in. Mud slides, brush fires, coastal erosion, earthquakes, mass killings, et cetera. We can relax and enjoy these disasters because in our hearts we feel that California deserves whatever it gets. Californians invented the concept of life-style. This alone warrants their doom." (65–66)

Suppose for the first "California" we substitute "Chernobyl," for the second we substitute "Russia," for "Californians" we substitute "Russians," and for "life-style" we substitute

"Communist revolution." Or this series of substitutions: "Hiroshima," "Japan," "Japanese," and "Greater East Asia Co-Prosperity Sphere." Or, in our imaginary scenario, "nuclear devastation of Tehran," "Iran," "Iranians," and "revolutionary Islamic fundamentalism." As both Baudrillard and Eco argue, in the cultural space of hyperreality, the distinction between the real and the simulated, the real and the fake, is blurred, and with that blurring, I would argue, comes a distancing which is conducive to the fascination which DeLillo's characters experience as they witness disasters through the medium of television.

NOTE

10. Don DeLillo, *White Noise* (New York: Viking, 1985). Hereafter cited in the text.

—Michael W. Messmer, "'Thinking it Through Completely': The Interpretation of Nuclear Culture." *The Centennial Review* 32, no. 4 (Fall 1988): pp. 402–404.

JOHN FROW ON THE CONSTRUCTION OF TYPICALITY IN THE NOVEL

[John Frow is the author of *Marxism and Literary History* (1986), *Cultural Studies and Cultural Value* (1995), and *Time and Commodity Culture: Essays in Cultural Theory and Postmodernity* (1997). In this excerpt, Frow discusses the ways in which DeLillo's work collapses the traditional novelistic opposition between detail and generality.]

In a town there are houses, plants in bay windows. People notice dying better. The dead have faces, automobiles. If you don't know a name, you know a street name, a dog's name. "He drove an orange Mazda." You know a couple of useless things about a person that become major facts of identification and cosmic placement when he dies suddenly, after a short illness, in his own bed, with a comforter and matching pillows, on a rainy Wednesday afternoon, feverish, a little congested in the sinuses and chest, thinking about his dry cleaning.

White Noise is obsessed with one of the classical aims of the realist novel: the construction of typicality. What this used to mean was a continuous process of extrapolation from the particular to the general, a process rooted in the existence of broad social taxonomies, general structures of human and historical destiny. Social typicality precedes the literary type—which is to say that the type is laid down in the social world; it is prior to and has a different kind of reality from secondary representations of it. First there is life, and then there is art. In *White Noise*, however, it's the other way round: social taxonomies are a function not of historical necessity but of style. Consider this description of the parents of Jack Gladney's students:

> The conscientious suntans. The well-made faces and wry looks. They feel a sense of renewal, of communal recognition. The women crisp and alert, in diet trim, knowing people's names. Their husbands content to measure out the time, distant but ungrudging, accomplished in parenthood, something about them suggesting massive insurance coverage.

This type is not a naive given, an embodied universality, but a self-conscious enactment; the middle-class parents know the ideality they are supposed to represent, and are deliberately living up to it. But this means that the type loses its purity, since it can always be imitated, feigned; or rather that there is no longer a difference in kind between the social category and the life-style which brings it into everyday being: the type ceaselessly imitates itself—through the ritual assembly of station wagons, for example, which "tells the parents they are a collection of the like-minded and the spiritually akin, a people, a nation."

It is thus no longer possible to distinguish meaningfully between a generality embedded in life and a generality embedded in representations of life. The communal recognition that constitutes the social class is part of a more diffuse system of recognitions conveyed through an infinitely detailed network of mediations. When Jack tries to characterize the convicted murderer his son Heinrich plays chess with, he draws on a range of mass-cultural information, like those psychological "profiles" that construct, above all for television, a taxonomy of criminal types: "Did he care for his weapons obsessively? Did he have an arsenal stacked in his shabby little room off a six-story concrete car park?" A computer operator "had a skinny neck and jug-handle ears to go with his starved skull—the innocent prewar look of a rural murderer." Those who would be affected by the airborne toxic event would be "people who live in mobile homes out in the scrubby parts of the county, where the fish hatcheries are." The type of the bigot, embodied in Murray Siskind's landlord, is "very good with all those little tools and fixtures that people in cities never know the names of," and tends to drive a panel truck "with an extension ladder on the roof and some kind of plastic charm dangling from the rearview mirror." The whole of this world is covered by a fine grid of typifications, so detailed and precise that it preempts and contains contingency.

If the type is susceptible to minute description, then the traditional novelistic tension between detail and generality falls away, and Lukács's account of typicality becomes unworkable. For Lukács, typicality is best embodied in the category of particularity (*Besonderheit*), which stands midway between philosophical generality (*Allgemeinheit*) and descriptive detail, or singularity (*Einzelheit*); in a postmodern economy of mediations, however, where representations of generality suffuse every pore of the world, the opposition between the general and the singular collapses as they merge into a single, undialectical unity. The *petit fait vrai* of the realist novel, the meaningless detail whose sole function is to establish a realism effect, is no longer meaningless. Reconstructing the scene of his wife's adultery, Jack mentions objects like "the fire-retardant carpet" and "the rental car keys on the dresser"; the definite article here marks these— as it does in much of Auden's poetry—not as concrete particulars but as generic indicators; they are not pieces of detail broken off from the contingent real but fragments of a mundane typicality.

—John Frow, "The Last Things Before the Last: Notes on *White Noise*." *The South Atlantic Quarterly* 89, no. 2 (Spring 1990): pp. 415–417.

N. H. REEVE AND RICHARD KERRIDGE ON WILDER'S UNCONTAMINATED TRUST

[N. H. Reeve and Richard Kerridge are the coeditors of *Nearly Too Much: The Poetry of J.H. Prynne* (1995). N. H. Reeve is the author of *The Novels of Rex Warner: An Introduction* (1989), and Richard Kerridge is the coeditor of Writing the Environment: Ecocriticism and Literature (1998) with Neil Sammells. In this excerpt, Reeve and Kerridge interpret Wilder's naïve tricycle ride across the expressway as the antithesis to Jack's paranoia.]

In the closing chapter of the novel, the narrative momentum generated by Jack's unsuccessful plot against his panic gives way to a series of interchangeable sequences. It is as if once death has both implanted itself in consciousness, and defied the best efforts of language to secure it, existence is free to revert to its former guise, as a succession of self-contained, minor, temporary panics, each with its 'whirling miscellany' of 'vivid textures and connections' (p. 313), and each more or less rapidly assuaged. The anxiety for control which had driven Jack on, towards knowledge and murder, or towards hosting his Hitler conference, is set in these last episodes against various other forms of reaction.

First of all Wilder, Babette's four-year-old son, rides his tricycle straight across the motorway, in a kind of crystallisation of all the previous disruptions of the regular flow of life. Wilder is the figure who trusts absolutely, with the heedless commitment to the immediate moment that his parents try vainly to recover for themselves. He stands at the polar opposite to the paranoid suspicion that always seeks for an overt or hidden route between the things it encounters:

> The world was a series of fleeting gratifications. He took what he could, then immediately forgot it in the rush of a subsequent pleasure. It was this forgetfulness I envied and admired. (p. 170)

Wilder's unwitting adventure among the cars, with its narrow, seemingly miraculous avoidance of death and its last-minute rescue by a quick-thinking driver, constructs a new frame for the interplay of old antagonisms: vulnerable flesh against hard metal, child against adult, the dull security of the flow against the liberating danger of departure from it. The scene becomes an illustration of the social and psychological characteristics that Sister Hermann Marie had outlined, as it draws out of its observers so much of their latent desire to protect and be protected, the 'uncontrollable terror' (p. 324) of their own helplessness, the sudden relief as a comforting power stoops down and saves. The sense that children somehow have an 'exemption from harm' (p. 289), as Murray puts it, brings into focus the adult's sense of loss:

'The child is everything, the adult nothing. Think about it. A person's entire life is the unraveling of this conflict.' (p. 290)

But simultaneously as the unself-conscious life, without fear or memory, is presented as the longed-for alternative negotiation with postmodern conditions, it is also what unmistakeably qualifies one to be the ideal late-capitalist consumer:

I always feel good when I'm with Wilder. Is it because pleasures don't cling to him? He is selfish without being grasping, selfish in a totally unbounded and natural way. There's something wonderful about the way he drops one thing, grabs for another. (p. 209)

The progress of modern capitalism has increasingly come to depend upon the shortening of shelf-life, the most rapid replacement possible of one product with another. This may register in various ways, from the built-in obsolescence of consumer goods, to the relatively recent emphasis on the corporate production of deliberately ephemeral spectacles and events. Large economic and political interests are at stake in the fomenting of a form of schizophrenia, whereby different experiences of consumption are presented as if they were radically disconnected from each other, and answered to the demands of differentiated selves which could never be permanently satisfied. Clearly the lightness of attachment to things which the child exemplifies, and which enables Jack, under the foreboding of his own mortality, to recover in Wilder's company some of his earlier sense of well-being, is consistently implicated in the continuity of certain capitalist practices. Jack's ascription, moreover, of some transcendent significance to this engagement with replaceability, in adjectives like 'unbounded' and 'natural', instead of denoting an authentic ground, seems to illustrate something akin to what Habermas called the 'longing for an undefiled, immaculate and stable present', concealed in precisely the value placed by the postmodern world on the transitory and the fleeting—either by way of a conservatism by which evanescence paradoxically becomes a permanent condition, or by way of a sentimental idealising of whatever does not survive long enough to lose its purity and become contaminated.

—N. H. Reeve and Richard Kerridge, "Postmodernism and DeLillo's *White Noise.*" *The Cambridge Quarterly* 23, no. 4 (1994): pp. 318–320.

CYNTHIA DEITERING ON TOXIC CONSCIOUSNESS IN THE NOVEL

[Cynthia Deitering has taught at Indian University-Purdue University at Fort Wayne and the University of Michigan. In this excerpt, Deitering interprets Jack Gladney's inspection of the family garbage as an example of a new "toxic consciousness" in fiction.]

During the 1980s—the decade that began amid anxious speculation about long-term consequences of the nuclear accident at Three Mile Island and drew to a close amid congressional hearings on the greenhouse effect—U.S. novelists showed an increasing concern with the pervasive problem of toxic waste, a concern that is reflected in what I propose to be a new "toxic consciousness" in recent American fiction. Fiction of the 1980s, in its sustained and various representations of pollution, offers insight into a culture's shifting relation to nature and to the environment at a time when the imminence of ecological collapse was, and is, part of the public mind and of individual imaginations. This paper first offers a brief descriptive survey of recent American fiction in order to illustrate a progressive preoccupation with what British novelist Martin Amis has called the "toiletization of the planet"; it then speculates on these texts as they mirror a shift in our cultural identity—a shift from a culture defined by its production to a culture defined by its waste; lastly, it examines the way in which the toxic landscape functions in these novels as a metaphor for the pollution of the natural world, and attempts to show how that contamination inevitably transmogrifies one's experience of the earth itself.

In 1982, prior to the toxic catastrophe of the Union Carbide incident in Bhopal, India, and in what now seems an age of relative innocence in regard to the global contamination of the environment, three of the year's most notable novels thematized, to some extent, a concern with the poisoning of the American landscape. In Saul Bellow's *The Dean's December*, the protagonist is asked by an eminent geophysicist to collaborate on a project to set before the public apocalyptic evidence that three industrial centuries of lead dispersal into the air, water and soil have resulted in the stupefaction of the West. John Cheever's final novella, *Oh What a Paradise It Seems*, focuses on an aging protagonist's symbolic efforts to restore Beazley's Pond—now a toxic dumpsite—to its original purity. And in John Gardner's *Mickelsson's Ghosts* (also a final novel), Peter Mickelsson's newly purchased farmhouse in a remote mountain community turns out to be contaminated by illegally dumped chemicals. By the mid 1980s, this concern with chemical contamination had become a novelistic preoccupation, figuring as an important theme in texts such as Don DeLillo's *White Noise*, Walker Percy's *The Thanatos Syndrome*, Paul Theroux's *O-Zone*, T. Coraghessan Boyle's *World's End*, and Richard Russo's *Mohawk*, and figuring, too, as an important subtext in such novels as Saul Bellow's *More Die of Heartbreak*, Margaret Arwood's *The Handmaid's Tale*, and William Gaddis' *Carpenter's Gothic*. Although a tendency toward apocalyptic themes may be partly due to the historical moment— "the countdown to a millennium"—a preoccupation with the toxic environment in American fiction of the 1980s seems to involve more than millennial ethos. Rather, toxic waste seems to function in recent fiction both as cultural metaphor for a society's most general fears about its collective future and as expression of an ontological rupture in its perception of the Real.

What I see as a new "toxic consciousness" in fiction reflects a fundamental shift in historical consciousness; for at some point during the Reagan–Bush decade, something happened, some boundary was crossed beyond which Americans perceived themselves differently in their relation to the natural world and the ecosystems of the American Empire. What happened, I believe, is that we came to perceive, perhaps inchoately, our own complicity in postindustrial ecosystems, both personal and national, which are predicated on pollution and waste. My premise is that during the 1980s we began to perceive ourselves as inhabitants of a culture defined by its waste, and that a number of American novels written during this period reflect this ontological transformation. I shall illustrate my point here chiefly through two novels, Don DeLillo's *White Noise* and John Updike's *Rabbit at Rest*.

White Noise, published in 1985, depicts a society whose most distinguishing feature is its waste. In the following passage, DeLillo's narrator, Jack Gladney, sifts through his family's compacted garbage, speculating about this middle-class domestic glut as the underside of consumer capitalism:

> I jabbed at it with the butt end of a rake and then spread the material over the concrete floor. I picked through it item by item, mass by shapeless mass, wondering why I felt guilty, a violator of privacy, uncovering intimate and perhaps shameful secrets. It was hard not to be distracted by some of the things they'd chosen to submit to the Juggernaut appliance. But why did I feel like a household spy? Is garbage so private? Does it glow at the core with a personal heat, with signs of one's deepest nature, clues to secret yearnings, humiliating flaws? What habits, fetishes, addictions, inclinations? What solitary acts, behavioral ruts? ... I found a banana skin with a tampon inside. Was this the dark underside of consumer consciousness?

By fathoming his family's garbage, it seems, Gladney might fathom not only the consciousness of consumer capitalism, but also the individual identities of his wife and children. By understanding the forms of their trash, he might glimpse their true selves as idiosyncratic producers of waste. Here the familiar notion of finding one's identity in commodity products is transformed into the notion of finding one's identity not in the commodities themselves but in their configuration as waste products. A similar transformation is reflected in Gladney's descriptions of the commodities he purchases and eventually discards. Though he feels himself "grow in value and self worth" as a result of these purchases, it is nonetheless only when he ferrets through the house looking for commodity objects to throw away that he uses language which connects his identity to the commodities he owns. In other words, it is when these commodities are perceived as trash that he sees them as extensions of himself, discarding them while "trying to say goodby to himself." DeLillo's characterization here of a man who is, in one sense, defined by his garbage capsulizes this new shift in ontological representation I have suggested. In a postindustrial economy which depends upon the expeditious transformation of goods into waste (thereby enabling the quick purchase of replacement goods), we have come to see in our garbage parts of ourselves, of our personal histories. On some level, perhaps, we have begun to comprehend our seminal role as producers of waste.

—Cynthia Deitering, "The Postnatural Novel: Toxic Consciousness in Fiction of the 1980s." *The Ecocriticism Reader: Landmarks in Literary Ecology*, ed. Cheryll Glotfelty and Harold Fromm, (Athens, Georgia: The University of Georgia Press, 1996): pp. 196–197, 198.

THOMAS PEYSER ON THE SHADOW OF GLOBALIZATION IN A DOMESTIC, WHITE NOVEL

[Thomas Peyser is the author of *W.W.* (a novel) and *Utopia and Cosmopolis: Globalization in the Era of American Literary Realism* (1998). In this excerpt, Peyser argues that the novel's culturally homogeneous setting serves DeLillo's project of critiquing the staid element of society that is threatened by globalization.]

There is nothing new about globalization, if by that we mean the patching together of different regions of the earth through economic and cultural exchange or political domination and alliance. Immanuel Wallerstein, whose book *The Modern World-System* marks an important point of departure for recent thought on globalization, argues that the system became firmly established in the sixteenth century, at which time European hegemony began its long process of entrenchment.[2] Even were one to prefer some other moment as the starting point of a truly modern world-system, the brute fact of two world wars in this century is enough to suggest that the earth has been for some time undergoing a process of increasingly intense integration, an intensity that has been immeasurably enhanced and made an intimate fact of everyday life by advances in transportation and communication. What is new—startlingly and even shockingly new—is the sway that the idea of globality holds over the imagination, the force with which the processes and consequences of globalization impinge upon the individual mind. Thus, the decades following World War II have witnessed not only the emergence of what Frederick Buell describes as "a new, syncretic, hybridized media-based global culture,"[3] but also of intellectual and artistic attempts to re-conceive ideas of human association and culture, ideas whose foundations in the concept of bounded localities have been disrupted by what Roland Robertson calls "the crystallization of the globe as a single place."[4] One novelist who has consistently explored the ramifications of this "crystallization" is Don DeLillo, whose works often depict the pleasures and, more often, the hazards attending the new world order. *White Noise*, which in some ways seems the most "domestic" of DeLillo's recent novels, presents a disturbing vision of a thoroughly globalized America, an America whose cultural (and territorial) boundaries seem more and more to exist in theory only.

The urgency with which we need to interrogate visions like DeLillo's—that register the impact of globalization—is easy to understand: whether or not we welcome the accelerating tempo of globalization naturally depends on which imaginative conceptions of the unprecedentedly integrated global order strike us as convincing. This is the justification for Arjun Appadurai's claim that "imagination ... is the key component of the new global order," "a form of negotiation between sites of agency ('individuals') and globally defined fields of possibility."[5] We need, therefore, to think about novels (and other cultural productions) depicting a globalized world not simply because we can show that art is "grounded" in social circumstance, but because novels themselves may have a crucial role to play in the very process of globalization. This is not to say, of course, that the only things holding today's world-system together are imaginative constructs; we can be tolerably certain that all the imagination coupled with the best will in the world would not dissuade capital from its global quest for profit. Nevertheless, the future patterns traced by the flow of capital, culture, and political power will, to some extent, depend upon the way the global field is imagined by those acting as agents within it.

Those familiar with the range of DeLillo's work may find it odd to look at *White Noise* in this context. After all, such novels as *Players*, *The Names*, *Running Dog*, *Libra*, and *Mao II* all focus explicitly—some might say obsessively—on international terrorism and globetrotting expeditions (often spiralling in on the political morass of the Middle East). Some readers seem to think of *White Noise* as an exception to this pattern; John McClure's recent, provocative analysis of DeLillo's international theme does not even mention the novel.[6] It is not hard to explain this omission: *White Noise* is obstinately domestic; central characters talk about other countries without themselves budging more than a few miles from their homes in the American heartland.

If globalization really is a key to our position today, however, then we should expect even this heartland to be indelibly marked with traces of the global. Since globalization punctures old national and cultural boundaries, along with the comfort or sense of belonging they provided, there is really no need to seek its symptoms exclusively—or even especially—in the far-flung. Although it is natural that those of us interested in the concept of globalization should also be interested in writings set or from all over the world, this must not obscure the fact that, so to say, globalization begins at home—no matter where on the globe that home is. Indeed, Appadurai suggests that America is a privileged site of globalization, arguing that a meditation on the "postnational" "moves us ... to America, a postnational space marked by its whiteness but marked too by its uneasy engagement with diasporic peoples [and] mobile technologies."[7] Compared to many of DeLillo's novels, in fact, the whiteness of *White Noise* is striking; toward its conclusion the narrator is even told, "You are very white, you know that?"[8] The observation might be applied to the novel itself. In fact, however, DeLillo's uncharacteristically narrow focus on the privileged world of the white middle-class—exemplified in this novel by the academy—gives him the space to depict the way global forces impinge on old cultural boundaries and even how they disable the very concepts of boundedness and community.

2. See Immanuel Wallerstein, *The Modern World-System: Capitalist Agriculture and the Origins of the European World-Economy in the Sixteenth Century* (New York: Academic Press, 1974).

3. Frederick Buell, *National Culture and the New Global System* (Baltimore: Johns Hopkins UP, 1994), 5.

4. Roland Robertson, *Globalization: Social Theory and Global Culture* (London: Sage, 1992), 64.

5. Arjun Appadurai, "Disjuncture and Difference in the Global Cultural Economy," *Public Culture* 2 (1990): 5.

6. John McClure, "Systems and Secrets: Don DeLillo's Postmodern Thrillers," *Late Imperial Romance* (New York: Verso, 1994), 118–51.

7. Arjun Appadurai, "Patriotism and Its Futures," *Public Culture* 5 (1993): 412.

8. Don DeLillo, *White Noise* (New York: Penguin, 1985), 310. Further references to this edition are noted parenthetically in the text.

—Thomas Peyser, "Globalization in America: The Case of Don DeLillo's *White Noise.*" *CLIO: A Journal of Literature, History and the Philosophy of History* 25, no. 3 (Spring 1996): pp. 255–257.

DANA PHILLIPS ON THE NOVEL AS "POSTMODERN PASTORAL"

[Dana Phillips has taught American literature at the University of Pennsylvania, Princeton University, and Bryn Mawr College, and has published articles on postmodernism and the environment. In this excerpt, Phillips calls the novel an expression of a blocked pastoral impulse.]

As a corrective to the prevailing critical views of the novel, *White Noise* might be seen as an example of what I will call the *postmodern pastoral*, in order to foreground the novel's surprising interest in the natural world and in a mostly forgotten and, indeed, largely bygone rural American landscape. At first glance the setting of the novel and its prevailing tone seem wholly unpastoral. But then the pastoral is perhaps the most plastic of modes, as William Empson demonstrated in *Some Versions of Pastoral.* The formula for "the pastoral process" proposed by Empson—"putting the complex into the simple" (23)—is one which might appeal to the main character and narrator of *White*

Noise, Jack Gladney. Gladney is someone who would like very much to put the complex into the simple, but who can discover nothing simple in the postmodern world he inhabits, a world in which the familiar oppositions on which the pastoral depends appear to have broken down. And thus the postmodern pastoral must be understood as a *blocked* pastoral—as the expression of a perpetually frustrated pastoral impulse or desire. In qualifying my assertion that *White Noise* is an example of postmodern pastoral in this way, I am trying to heed Paul Alpers's warning that "modern studies tend to use 'pastoral' with ungoverned inclusiveness" (ix). However, Alpers's insistence that "we will have a far truer idea of pastoral if we take its representative anecdote to be herdsmen and their lives, rather than landscape or idealized nature" (22) would prevent altogether the heuristic use of the term I wish to make here. With all due respect to herdsmen, the interest of the pastoral for me lies more in the philosophical debate it engenders about the proper relation of nature and culture and less in its report on the workaday details of animal husbandry or the love lives of shepherds.

Jack Gladney is not a shepherd, but a professor of Hitler Studies at the College-on-the-Hill, which is situated in the midst of an unremarkable sprawl of development that could be called "suburban," except that there is no urban center to which the little town of Blacksmith is subjoined. Like almost everything else in *White Noise*, the town, to judge from Jack Gladney's description of it, seems displaced, or more precisely, unplaced. Jack tells us that "Blacksmith is nowhere near a large city. We don't feel threatened and aggrieved in quite the same way other towns do. We're not smack in the path of history and its contaminations" (85). He proves to be only half-right: the town is, in fact, subject to "contaminations," historically and otherwise. Jack's geography is dated: Blacksmith is not so much "nowhere" as it is Everywhere, smack in the middle—if that is the right phrase—of a typically uncentered contemporary American landscape of freeways, airports, office parks, and abandoned industrial sites. According to Jack, "the main route out of town" passes through "a sordid gantlet of used cars, fast food, discount drugs and quad cinemas" (119). We've all run such a gantlet; we've all been to Blacksmith. It is the sort of town you can feel homesick for "even when you are there" (257).

Thus, despite a welter of detail, the crowded landscape in and around Blacksmith does not quite constitute a place, not in the sense of "place" as something that the characters in a more traditional novel might inhabit, identify with, and be identified by. Consider Jack's description of how Denise, one of the Gladney children, updates her "address" book: "She was transcribing names and phone numbers from an old book to a new one. There were no addresses. Her friends had phone numbers only, a race of people with a seven-bit analog consciousness" (41). Consciousness of place as something that might be geographically or topographically (that is, locally) determined has been eroded by a variety of more universal cultural forms in addition to the telephone. Chief among them is television—Jack calls the TV set the "focal point" of life in Blacksmith (85). These more universal cultural forms are not just forms of media and media technology, however; the category includes such things as, for example, tract housing developments.

Despite the prefabricated setting of *White Noise* and the "seven-bit analog consciousness" of its characters, an earlier, more natural and more pastoral landscape figures throughout the novel as an absent presence of which the characters are still dimly aware. Fragments of this landscape are often evoked as negative tokens of a loss the characters feel but cannot quite articulate, or more interestingly—and perhaps more postmodern as well—as negative tokens of a loss the characters articulate, but cannot quite feel. In an early scene, one of many in which Jack Gladney and his colleague Murray Jay Siskind ponder the "abandoned meanings" of the postmodern world (184), the two men visit "THE MOST PHOTOGRAPHED BARN IN AMERICA," which lies "twenty-two miles into the country around Farmington" (12). In his role as narrator, Jack Gladney often notes details of topography with what seems to be a specious precision. But the speciousness of such details is exactly the issue. Even though it is surrounded by a countrified landscape of "meadows and apple orchards" where fences trail through "rolling fields" (12), Farmington is not at all what its name still declares it to be: a farming town. The aptness of that place-name, and of the bits of rural landscape still surrounding the barn, has faded like an old photograph. As Murray Jay Siskind observes, "Once you've seen the signs about the barn, it becomes impossible to see the barn"

(12). The reality of the pastoral landscape has been sapped, not just by its repeated representation on postcards and in snapshots, but also by its new status as a tourist attraction: by the redesignation of its cow paths as people-movers. The question of authenticity, of originality, of what the barn was like "before it was photographed" and overrun by tourists, however alluring it may seem, remains oddly irrelevant (13). This is the case, as Murray observes, because he and Jack cannot get "outside the aura" of the cultural fuss surrounding the object itself, "the incessant clicking of shutter release buttons, the rustling crank of levers that advanced the film" (13)—noises that drown out the incessant clicking of insect wings and the rustling of leaves that once would have been the aural backdrop to the view of the barn.

—Dana Phillips, "Don DeLillo's Postmodern Pastoral." *Reading the Earth: New Directions in the Study of Literature and the Environment*, ed. Michael P. Branch et al., (Moscow, Idaho: University of Idaho Press, 1998): pp. 236–238.

TIM ENGLES ON RACIALIZED PERCEPTION IN THE NOVEL

[Tim Engles is an Assistant Professor in the Department of English at Eastern Illinois University and the coeditor of *Critical Essays on Don DeLillo* (2000). In this excerpt, Engles argues that the novel's protagonist Jack Gladney relies heavily on racial categories to construct his identity.]

As the novel begins, narrator and protagonist Jack Gladney describes an annual "spectacle" at the college where he works as a professor, "the day of the station wagons" (DeLillo, *White* 3). As he closely observes a long line of cars driven by parents dropping off their children, Jack detects among these people a sense of community grounded not in common values or interests, but rather in mutual recognition of familiar attitudes and poses: "The students greet each other with comic cries and gestures of sodden collapse. [...] Their parents stand sun-dazed near their automobiles, seeing images of themselves in every direction. The conscientious suntans. The well-made faces and wry looks. They feel a sense of renewal, of communal recognition" (3). DeLillo immediately highlights here the narcissistic nature of the connections the people in this novel tend to register between each other. The people in this scene would seem content merely because they are among others who are like themselves, but Jack recognizes more precisely the foundations of their sense of community. These parents and their children actually appreciate the presence of others who are like themselves because, in looking at these familiar others, they see themselves. As Jack recognizes, they also base their "sense of communal recognition" on a flood of products, including the "bicycles, skis, rucksacks, English and Western saddles, inflated rafts, [...] the stereo sets, radios and personal computers; small refrigerators and table ranges, [...] the junk food still in shopping bags—onion-and-garlic-chips, nacho thins, peanut creme patties, Waffelos and Kabooms, fruit chews and toffee popcorn; the Dum-Dum pops, the Mystic mints" (3). Jack's use of the definite article here signals his weary familiarity with these objects, and with this "spectacle," which he has "witnessed [...] every September for twenty-one years" (3). But the familiarity of these items is crucial to the communal bond among these people, for, in seeing others who also own them, they can categorize such people as like themselves, thereby categorizing themselves as well. Indeed, as Jack notes, because so much is on display here, this "assembly of station wagons, as much as anything they might do in the course of the year, more than formal liturgies or laws, tells the parents they are a collection of the like-minded and the spiritually akin, a people, a nation" (4).

DeLillo thus establishes immediately the novel's interest in the relational, dialogic nature of identity formation, showing that our perception of others necessarily relies on categorical placement in relation to categorical placement of oneself. Subsequent examples of this phenomenon include the implicit assertion of the white self via the explicit recognition of "non-white" others; such moments show that in order to assert themselves, implicitly white individuals, like members of other, more marked categories, rely symbiotically for their conceptions of self on the categories of people that have developed in this country. DeLillo eventually demonstrates that in racial terms, members of the "white race" tend to rely on racialized categories for "non-whites" when regarding them, but not when regarding other whites. They thus seem to escape such categorization themselves when regarded by the dominant (that is, white) gaze (and certainly not, much to their probable surprise, when regarded by the gaze of an overtly racialized other).

Of course, as time goes by and American racial formations continue to mutate, generational differences in habitual deployment of racial categories evince themselves. DeLillo's portraits in *White Noise* of variously aged characters periodically reflect such changes. At one point, Jack and his fourteen-year-old son Heinrich demonstrate such a difference in their perceptions of an apparently "non-white" other, Heinrich's friend Orest Mercator. As the three of them chat together on the front steps of the Gladney home, Jack is befuddled by Orest's plans to enter the record books by sitting for sixty-seven days in a cage full of poisonous snakes. Heinrich is struck with admiration, and he seems not to mind that his friend's skin is distinctly darker than his, nor that his race is difficult to discern. Jack, on the other hand, tries to get a fix on this "older boy [...] of uncertain pigmentation" by attempting to insert him into familiar racial categories (DeLillo, *White* 206). "What kind of name is Orest?" Jack wonders, studying his features: "He might have been Hispanic, Middle Eastern, Central Asian, a dark-skinned Eastern European, a light-skinned black. Did he have an accent? I wasn't sure. Was he a Samoan, a native North American, a Sephardic Jew? It was getting hard to know what you couldn't say to people" (208). Jack's colloquial usage of an indefinite "you" here refers implicitly to a white audience. His complaint acknowledges that white people accustomed to easily categorizable others are often at a loss in the face of the contemporary influx of immigrants, who could be from almost anywhere. As part of a gradual awakening to his habitual reliance on perceptual categories, Jack becomes vaguely aware, as he is here with Orest Mercator (whose cartographically resonant name evokes "the rest of the world"), of the eroding reliability of traditional American racial categories. Nevertheless, Jack has been raised as an implicitly white person in a culture bolstered by iconographic celebrations of heroic white men acting out their individualized roles against a backdrop of "inferior," racialized others. Thus, he eventually reverts to habitual uses of racialized others, casting them as bit players within his own similar enactments of a received, white male fantasy of selfhood. Prior to portraying Jack doing so, DeLillo establishes his protagonist's more general reliance on habitual categories to conceive of others, thereby implicitly registering a relational, falsely individualistic conception of himself.

—Tim Engles, "'Who Are You, Literally?': Fantasies of the White Self in *White Noise*." *Modern Fiction Studies* 45, no. 3 (Fall 1999): pp. 761–763.

MARION MUIRHEAD ON THE NOVEL'S NARRATIVE LOOPS

[Marion Muirhead has published articles in *Critique, Southern Literary Journal*, and Dracula: *The Shade and the Shadow*: A Critical Anthology (1998). In this excerpt, Muirhead draws on fractal geometry to explain the novel's plot structure, as represented by the piece of twine in Jack's garbage.]

Critics have noted the presence of a piece of string in the garbage under investigation; its description suggests an allusion to plot structure and interpretation:

There was a long piece of twine that contained a series of knots and loops. It seemed at first a random construction. Looking more closely I thought I detected a complex relationship between the size of the loops, the degree of the knots (single or double) and the intervals between the knots with loops and freestanding knots. Some kind of occult geometry or symbolic festoon of obsessions. (258–59)

The reading process requires a search for patterns, and a mind conditioned to search for such patterns can find them almost anywhere. Resistant to the very idea of plots and avoiding them in his life wherever possible, Jack still cannot help finding them in the abstract. The knot is a traditional figure for the complication in narrative, a mystery that must be unraveled or a mystical tie that binds. Knots and loops decorate the pages of ancient texts, especially *The Book of Kells* with its interlace designs found in the Anglo-Saxon tradition. Loops signify repetition in narrative events, feedback iterations, here occurring on multiple levels suggested by the different sizes of the loops in the twine. Tom LeClair asserts that the movements of characters from place to place, to Iron City and back, represent loops, as do their habits as consumers—purchasing, consuming, discarding, and purchasing again. LeClair states, "Like other systems novelists, DeLillo recycles American waste into art to warn against entropy, both thermodynamic and informational" (212). The assertion that waste is recycled into art recalls the memorable tampon within a banana skin in Jack's board of refuse and suggests narrative embedding of the unexpected kind. It is entirely reasonable to expect to find a banana inside a banana skin or, alternatively, nothing; the presence of a tampon suggests a breakdown in the expected order, an entropic miscegenation of waste.

Narrative embedding can be modeled effectively in the mapping of chaotic processes. Self-similarity occurs when a mathematical function is repeated on scales of different lengths, resulting in a proliferation of forms such as the fern-like tendrils of the Julia Set or the bud-like shapes of the Mandelbrot set. Self-affinity occurs when, during feedback iterations, the proportions of the form as well as the scale length alter. This process can be illustrated with the example of forms found in periculture. The formal shape of a perfect round pearl is an example of self-similarity: layers of nacre build up in stages around a nucleus; and those layers correspond to feedback iterations in which only the scale changes, becoming larger as the process unfolds. A baroque pearl, however, has a more or less irregular shape and its proportions as well as its scale may change. A formal narrative in which events are predictable develops from a process like that of the round pearl, whereas an unpredictable narrative of complexity may, in its structure, resemble the baroque pearl, which may take a rare or even a unique form (Joyce and Addison 65–70).

There is, interestingly, a fairly rare form of pearl known as the cruciform or x-shaped baroque, a shape that suggests bifurcation, an important principle both in narrative and in mathematics. A bifurcation point indicates a change in the mathematical function that determines the form. In a dissipative structure, the bifurcation point is also the point of maximum entropy from which a new form emerges. As in thermodynamics, entropy is usually associated with a breakdown of recognizable patterning, but in chaotics entropy has been viewed, more recently, as a creative factor. The pearl, an object of beauty, develops from a foreign irritant injected into the mollusk's body, and the secretions that the oyster uses to protect itself are actually waste products. The recycling of waste into art occurs on an organic level in the mollusk; in *White Noise*, it occurs on the machinic level.

The loop as an emblem of nonlinear fractal iteration and reiteration in a narrative contrasts with the more traditional metaphor of multiple strands being pulled together and woven into a linear pattern, text as textile; both tropes can suggest complexity. In a novel with several separate but converging plot lines that are woven into a fabric in which the relevance of each strand to the other resonates analeptically, the obsessive search for patterns is rewarded when these strands converge and the reader's hypothesis is proven or disproven. An informational model to supplant that of the textile is provided by the process of mathematical convergence, which occurs when feedback iterations progressively approach a particular integer (Peitgen 265). This integer is the solution to the mathematical problem, just as the resolution of the plot solves the reader's dilemma.

—Marion Muirhead, "Deft Acceleration: The Occult Geometry of Time in *White Noise*." *Critique: Studies in Contemporary Fiction* 42, no. 4 (Summer 2001): pp. 404–405.

Underworld

Underworld is primarily the story of Nick Shay and his experiences from the early 1950's through the early 1990's. DeLillo presents the narrative, however, in reverse chronological order, so that Nick's present identity and his past are inverted. This experimental narrative technique blurs the boundaries of time and space and highlights the slippery relationship between cause and effect in the postmodern world.

Meanwhile, the narrative of Manx Martin remains fixed on one day in 1951, chronicling his decision to steal a homerun baseball from his son and sell it.

The prologue, entitled "The Triumph of Death," recounts the famous baseball game between the New York Giants and the Brooklyn Dodgers at the Polo Grounds in the Bronx on October 3, 1951. Cotter Martin, a 14 year-old Harlem boy, sneaks into the game and outruns security. J. Edgar Hoover, director of the CIA, attends the game in the company of the reveling Jackie Gleason, Frank Sinatra and Toots Shor. Midway through the game, J. Edgar Hoover hears from Special Agent Rafferty that the Soviets have conducted their second atomic test. Toward the end of the game, Hoover finds amongst the debris two pages torn from *Life* magazine that feature a reproduction of Pieter Brueghel's 16th century painting *The Triumph of Death*. Awed by the spectacle of death attacking life, he saves it. When George Thomson hits the homerun that wins the game for the Giants, the ball flies into the stands and Cotter Martin wins the fight for it, taking it home.

In Part One ("Long Tall Sally: Spring-Summer 1992"), Nick Shay, a 57 year-old former New Yorker who has been relocated to Phoenix, Arizona, locates a former lover of his, the now famous artist Klara Sax. She is painting deactivated military aircraft—planes that once carried nuclear bombs. Nick returns to his home in Phoenix, where he works at a waste handling firm which disposes of radioactive plutonium, and his close friends in the firm are Brian Glassic and Simeon Biggs (Big Sims).

Nick reflects on the word plutonium, which comes from Pluto, the god of the dead and ruler of the underworld. One night, he wakes up from a nightmare and sits up in an armchair holding one of his prized possessions: the homerun ball that Thomson supposedly hit on that day in 1951. But Nick, a Dodger fan, has bought it as the losing ball—the ball that represents the bad luck of the number 13, the sheer power of misfortune. Nick is haunted by the memory of his father, Jimmy Costanza, a bookmaker who disappeared going out to buy cigarettes when Nick was 11 years old.

The next section is entitled "Manx Martin" after Cotter Martin's father. Cotter shows his father the ball he caught at the baseball game, and Manx begins thinking of ways to sell it. Cotter refuses, insisting he wants to keep the ball. That night as Cotter sleeps, Manx steals the ball and leaves.

Part Two, entitled "Elegy for Left Hand Alone: Mid 1980s–Early 1990s" begins through the eyes of a home video camera in the hands of a little girl: the "video kid" who accidentally filmed one of the victims of the famous "Texas Highway Killer" as he was being killed. On a business trip, Brian Glassic visits Marvin Lundy, a baseball memorabilia collector in New Jersey who owns the ball that Thomson hit to win against the Dodgers in 1951. Some time later, Marvin receives a call from a "friend" of Brian (Nick Shay) who wants to buy the ball.

Nick visits his mother Rosemary and his younger brother Matty in the Bronx, his birthplace. While Nick believes his father was killed by the mafia, Matty maintains that he simply abandoned the family. Matty visits Albert Bronzini, his former chess mentor. Bronzini was once married to Klara Sax. Matty also sees Sister Edgar, a severe nun who once taught grade school but now administers aid to the needy at "The Wall," a tenement in the South Bronx whose side wall is spray-painted by famous graffiti writer Ismael Munoz, or "Moonman 157." Nick leaves town, while Brian and Nick's wife Marian continue an affair that has been going on for some time.

In Part Three, "The Cloud of Unknowing: Spring 1978" Nick has recently been hired to work for Waste Containment and meets Simeon Biggs, his unofficial advisor, at a business conference in Mojave Springs. Nick has an affair with a woman named Donna who is at the hotel for a swingers' convention. In a moment of emotional infidelity, he tells Donna something he never told his wife: when he was seventeen, he killed a man named George Manza. Upon returning home, Nick admits the affair to Marian. Meanwhile, Marvin Lundy and his wife are in San Francisco trying to track down Chuckie Wainwright, the man who owns the 1951 homerun baseball.

In the "Manx Martin" section that follows, we return again to 1951, when Manx goes to Yankee stadium in the middle of the night. Fans are lined up to buy tickets for the big game between the Giants and the Yankees, and he intends to find a buyer for the ball he has stolen from his son.

Following this section is Part Four, "Cocksucker Blues: Summer 1974" in which Klara Sax is 54 and between art projects. She accompanies Esther Winship, her dealer, in her search for Moonman 157 in the Bronx. Esther hopes to harness his graffiti talent in the art world, but he is untraceable.

In Part Five, "Better Things for Better Living Through Chemistry: Selected Fragments Public and Private in the 1950s and 1960s," Nick is in a correctional facility for juveniles as a result of killing George Manza, after which he is sent to Minnesota to be educated by the Jesuits. Following that, he has a two-year affair with Amy Brookhiser, who ends up having an abortion. Meanwhile, the comic Lenny Bruce chronicles the Cuban missile crisis of 1962 from beginning to end in his "spoken jazz" (586). Marian Bowman, who will later become Nick's wife, visits her mother in Madison Wisconsin, where there are major protests against Vietnam and against Dow Chemical for making a new improved form of napalm. In New York, protesters heckle the Black and White Ball at the Plaza Hotel, which is attended by J. Edgar Hoover, director of the CIA. Chuckie Wainwright, recalling his father giving him the 1951 homerun baseball, feels guilty because he either lost it or threw it away. Nick leaves a bar on the Lower East Side during the great "blackout" of November 9, 1965, and walks back to the Bronx, where he is staying in a hotel. Three years later he marries Marian, and five years later their son is born.

"Manx Martin" follows this character once again as he sells the famous baseball to Charles Wainwright while the man is waiting in line with his son Chuckie to buy Giants/Yankees tickets.

Part Six, "Arrangement in Gray and Black: Fall 1951-Summer 1952" returns full circle to the year of the novel's prologue. Albert Bronzini reads the front page of the newspaper, which proclaims that the Giants have captured the pennant against the Dodgers, and the USSR has exploded an atomic bomb. Nick Shay is sixteen and has dropped out of school, drives a stolen car, and frequents a poolroom where Mike the Book and George the Waiter (George Manza) serve as surrogate fathers. Nick meets Klara, now married to Albert Bronzini, and has an extended affair with her. One day, George Manza shows Nick his sawed-off shotgun, telling him it is not loaded. Nick points it a George's head and shoots, killing him.

The last section, entitled "Epilogue: Das Kapital," brings the action up to date. Marian has confessed her affair with Brian to Nick, and Nick confronts Brian about it while the two are on a business trip together. Nick, now a waste analyst, returns to Phoenix on more intimate terms with Marian than ever. Sister Edgar and Gracie still visit The Wall, searching for a girl named Esmerelda who lives wild among the rubble there. Finally they learn that Esmerelda has been raped and pushed off a roof. Ismael Munoz memorializes her in graffiti, and Edgar and Gracie join crowds of people who gather on a traffic island in the South Bronx to witness an apparition of Esmerelda, Lourdes-like, on the corner of a billboard advertising orange juice. Soon after, Sister Edgar dies in her sleep.

Underworld

Cotter Martin is a fourteen year-old black boy from the Bronx who sneaks into the Polo Grounds on the day of the big playoff game between the New York Giants and the Brooklyn Dodgers on October 3, 1951. He retrieves and takes home the baseball that Thomson hits into the stands to win the game for the Giants.

J. Edgar Hoover is the director of the CIA and one of the major players in the cold war between the United States and the Soviet Union. He is a target for protesters in the 1960s.

Nick Shay is a native of the Bronx, New York, who at age 16 kills an older man named George Manza. This takes his life on an unexpected trajectory, through a correctional facility and a Jesuit education, ending in Phoenix, Arizona with his wife Marian and two children. He works at a waste-handling firm that disposes of plutonium and nuclear radiation.

Marian Shay, formerly Marian Bowman, is Nick's wife. She has an affair with Nick's friend Brian Glassic and eventually admits her infidelity to Nick.

Klara Sax is a famous New York City artist who at one time is married to Albert Bronzini and has a child with him. While married to Albert, she has an affair with sixteen year-old Nick Shay. The culmination of her artwork is a project entitled "Long Tall Sally" in which she paints a fleet of military planes that once carried nuclear bombs during the cold war.

Simeon Biggs, nicknamed "Big Sims," is Nick's co-worker at the waste handling firm. He designs waste dumping sites and acts as a mentor to Nick.

Brian Glassic is Nick's co-worker and close friend. He has an affair with Nick's wife Marian. When confronted by Nick about it, he denies it until he hears that Marian has already admitted it.

Manx Martin, Cotter Martin's wayward father, is the only character whose story remains set in 1951, the day of the baseball game between the Dodgers and the Giants. Manx steals the homerun baseball from his son while he sleeps and sells it to Charles Wainwright as he waits in line to buy World Series tickets.

Marvin Lundy is a sports memorabilia collector living in Cliffside Park, New Jersey. He sells Nick what is supposedly the homerun baseball hit by Thomson in 1951.

Matt Shay, nicknamed Matty, is Nick's younger brother. As a child he becomes an accomplished chess player; once grown up, he does weapons research and analysis in New Mexico for the U.S. government.

Sister Edgar is a severe, punishing nun with a germ phobia who is Matty Shay's teacher in grade school in the Bronx. After she retires from teaching, she frequents the ghettos of the South Bronx, bringing aid to residents of the tenement called "The Wall" and selling information about abandoned cars to Ismael Munoz.

Gracie is a nun and friend of Sister Edgar. The two visit The Wall together, and Gracie makes it her personal mission to rescue a young homeless girl named Esmerelda who lives wild among the trash.

Charles Wainwright is an advertising account supervisor on 5th avenue who once bought a collectible baseball from Manx Martin while standing in line for tickets to the 1951 World Series.

Chuckie Wainwright is Charles Wainwright's rebellious son. After his father passes the famous collectible baseball down to him, he loses it and feels guilty about it.

George Manza is a master pool shooter, a heroin addict, and the object of a young and fatherless Nick Shay's admiration. He shows Nick his sawed-off shotgun, telling him it is not loaded. Nick in turn points the gun at George's head and shoots, killing him.

Underworld

DAVID REMNICK ON JOHN CHEEVER'S INFLUENCE ON DELILLO

[The editor of the *New Yorker*, David Remnick is the author of several books, including the Pulitzer Prize winning *Lenin's Tomb: The Last Days of the Soviet Empire* (1993) and *Resurrection: The Struggle for a New Russia* (1997). He is the editor of *Life Stories: Profiles from The New Yorker* (2001). In this excerpt, Remnick explains author John Cheever's part in DeLillo's writing process.]

DeLillo did not map out the architecture of "Underworld" and then begin. The process was much more intuitive, mysterious, floundering. There was never an outline. The writing began with a twenty-five-thousand-word burst—a set piece, which became the novel's prologue. It opens with a black kid named Cotter Martin sneaking into the Polo Grounds and then, like a movie camera that widens its focus, takes in the crowd. The opening, which first appeared as a novella called "Pafko at the Wall" in *Harper's*, is one of the most extraordinary performances in contemporary American fiction. DeLillo is able to get the wise-guy interplay among the Hollywood biggies in Leo Durocher's private box (Gleason vomiting on Sinatra's lisle socks), the fears and pleasure of Cotter in his fugitive seat, the animal movements of the crowd, the action on the field, the city's ecstatic reactions beyond, even J. Edgar Hoover surreptitiously studying a small reproduction of a Brueghel painting ("the meatblood colors and massed bodies"). Hoover, sitting in his box, knows that while the game is being played the Soviet Union is secretly testing a nuclear weapon in Kazakhstan, and he thinks, What secret history are they writing? DeLillo's focus, his camera, seems to career around the ballpark, from scene to scene, face to face, mind to mind, taking it all in, as if at once. (...)

While the Giants were playing the Dodgers for the '51 pennant, DeLillo was in a dentist's office on Crotona Avenue in the Bronx. He was, naturally, a Yankees fan, so he was mainly waiting it out to see who the next National League victim would be. Thomson's homer was not for him what it was for Giants fans. But forty years later, as he read an anniversary account of the game in the newspaper, he began to think about the event, how it seemed unrepeatable, the communal joy of it married, as it was on the front page of the *Times* in 1951, to the nuclear explosion in Kazakhstan. "Somebody seemed to be wanting to tell me something here," DeLillo said to me.

For a long time, DeLillo has been interested in the passage in John Cheever's journals where he wrote, after attending a ballgame at Shea Stadium, "The task of an American writer is not to describe the misgivings of a woman taken in adultery as she looks out of a window at the rain but to describe 400 people under the lights reaching for a foul ball ... [or] the faint thunder as 10,000 people, at the bottom of the eighth, head for the exits. The sense of moral judgments embodied in a migratory vastness."

"I had no idea this would be a novel," DeLillo said. "All I wanted to do was write a fictional account of this ballgame, and, for the first time ever, I was writing something whose precise nature I could not gauge. I didn't know whether I was writing a short story, a short novel, or a novel. But I did know that the dimensions of the Polo Grounds were my boundaries. I had no idea that I would go beyond this until after I finished.

"The prologue is written with a sort of super-omniscience. There are sentences that may begin in one part of the ballpark and end in another. I wanted to open up the scene. They become sort of travel-happy; they travel from one person's mind to another. I did it largely because it was pleasurable. It was baseball itself that provided a kind of freedom that perhaps I hadn't quite experienced before. It was the game."

After the prologue, "Underworld" cuts to 1992 and begins to work backward through the years of the Cold War, so that the day of the game, October 3, 1951, and the day Nick Shay shoots the waiter, October 4, 1951, are separated by forty years of narrative. The mechanical device that travels through the narrative as it weaves back and forth in time is the baseball—the baseball that Bobby Thomson hit into the seats at the Polo Grounds, the ball that Cotter Martin grabs and takes home, the ball that collectors, Nick Shay included, covet as a talisman of history. The ball is a kind of grail. Many of DeLillo's old themes are in "Underworld": the increasing power of the image and the media in the modern world; the uncertainty of American life after the Kennedy assassination; a sense of national danger; men and women who live outside the mainstream of ordinary life and language: There is even the whiff, here and there, of that most singular DeLillo trademark: paranoia. But, more often, "Underworld" is a darkly funny satire of postwar language, manner, and obsessions.

> —David Remnick, "Exile on Main Street." *The New Yorker* 15 September 1997: p. 44.

JAMES WOLCOTT ON DELILLO'S PORTRAYAL OF LENNY BRUCE

[James Wolcott is a contributing editor at *Vanity Fair*. In this excerpt, Wolcott praises DeLillo's portrayal of Lenny Bruce and the subculture he represents.]

Thematically, DeLillo has his ducks in a row. (He always does.) Like Norman Mailer in *Harlot's Ghost*, DeLillo is composing a psychological symphony of Cold War worry, a secret history of betrayal, paranoia, espionage, and military escalation smoothed over by official lies and *Reader's Digest* pieties. We American dupes brush our teeth a shiny white as our individuality rots at the root in the death ray of TV. Interestingly, both novels resurrect the standup comic Lenny Bruce to play the imp of the perverse, whose sick jokes and cackling laugh cut like Zorro through the cardigan sweaters of *Father Knows Best* family values. Comparing Mailer's Lenny Bruce to DeLillo's—well, it's no contest. The scene in *Harlot's Ghost* where Lenny Bruce scandalizes the ruling-class wasps with his jabbering tongue (get your coat, Mildred, we're going) is so stiff and stagy it belongs on the History Channel. Mailer is unable to convey Bruce's pimpy swagger as a performer. DeLillo's Lenny Bruce is a true charismatic, a pasty golem who seems to possess an independent existence and a cold skin. In the spirit of Albert Goldman's pop biography *Ladies and Gentleman, Lenny Bruce!*, DeLillo seems to be channeling Bruce from some hip room in the hereafter: "Lenny was a handsome guy with dark hair and hooded eyes and he resembled a poolshark who'd graduated to deeper and sleazier schemes. His brows were set at a cosmopolitan arch that seemed to function as an open challenge to his hustler aspect—if you're dumb enough to believe my scam, that's *your* problem, schmucko."

When Lenny Bruce makes his first appearance in *Underworld*, it's at a night club in West Hollywood during the hairiest period of the Cuban missile crisis in 1962:

> The seating at the Troubadour consisted mainly of folding chairs and when enough people laughed there was a wheezy groan from the slats and hinges. And the audience sat there thinking, How real can the crisis be if we're sitting in a club on Santa Monica Boulevard going ha ha ha.
>
> *"We're all gonna die!"*
>
> Lenny loves the postexistential bent of this line. In his giddy shriek the audience can hear the obliteration of the idea of uniqueness and free choice. They can hear the replacement of human isolation by massive and unvaried ruin. His closest followers laugh the loudest. Their fan-fed vanity is gratified. They're included in Lenny's own incineration. All the Lennies. The personal junkie. The anti-hypocrite. The satirist and nose picker. Lenny the hipster fink. Lenny the ass mechanic, girl-spotting in hotel lobbies. Lenny the vengeance of the Lord.

Heard in a club in San Francisco a week later, the audience full of aging dharma bums, the same material seems to land off to the side. The beats in the audience are ahead of Bruce when it comes to thinking the unthinkable:

> The beats didn't need a missile crisis to make them think about the bomb. The bomb was their handiest reference to the moral squalor of America, the guilty place of smokestacks and robot corporations, Time-magazined and J. Edgar Hoovered, where people sat hunched over cups of coffee in a thousand rainswept truckstops on a jazz prairie, secret Trotskyites and sad nymphomaniacs with Buddhist pussies—things Lenny

made fun of. Lenny was showbiz, he was suited and groomed and cool and corrupt, the mortician-comic....

It's a nifty piece of pop criticism that DeLillo delivers, a personality analysis of the audience that sums up an entire social wave, the evocation of "rainswept truckstops on a jazz prairie," a snapshot marriage of Jack Kerouac and Robert Frank (Kerouac having written the foreword to Frank's *The Americans*). The Lenny Bruce sections showcase how attuned DeLillo is to the nervous system of every subculture he enters in *Underworld*, from swingers playing musical beds at a hotel to waste specialists talking shop. It's a legacy from the New Journalism, this Silly Putty ability to shape-shift and imitate anyone at will. Some of the best scenes in *Underworld* are like day-glo passages from Tom Wolfe played on a black-and-white TV: social observation decolorized into a grainy monochrome of nostalgia. ("It is all failing indelibly into the past," is how DeLillo describes the dying glory of that day at the Polo Grounds.) Where Wolfe is exhilarated by the coltish energies of capitalism, the giddy froth and reckless abandon, DeLillo (a less fun guy) is drawn to the dark, glacial agents of change—the submerged megatrends. Wolfe puts on fashion shows, DeLillo takes institutional readings. He can look at a glass tower and perceive that although it's hooked to the world through faxes and modems, it inevitably becomes a citadel unto itself: "The corporation is supposed to take us outside ourselves. We design these organized bodies to respond to the market, face foursquare into the world. But things tend to drift dimly inward."

—James Wolcott, "Blasts From the Past." *The New Criterion* 16, no. 4 (December 1997): 66–68.

TONY TANNER ON WASTE AND THE EPIPHANIC MOMENT

[Tony Tanner is the author of *Henry James and the Art of Nonfiction* (1995) and *The American Mystery: American Literature from Emerson to DeLillo* (2000). In this excerpt, Tanner argues that DeLillo's novel does not successfully create the waste-inspired epiphanies it describes.]

Nick Shay is professionally involved with waste, which, perhaps not very subtly, allows for heaps of the stuff in the novel. "My firm was involved in waste. We were waste handlers, waste traders, cosmologists of waste.... Waste is a religious thing." He lives it; he thinks it. He and his wife "saw products as garbage even when they sat gleaming on store shelves, yet unbought." His workmate Brian goes to a landfill site on Staten Island: "He looked at all that soaring garbage and knew for the first time what his job was all about.... To understand all this. To penetrate this secret.... He saw himself for the first time as a member of an esoteric order." Another workmate, Big Sims, complains that, now, "Everything I see is garbage."

> "You see it everywhere because it is everywhere."
> "But I didn't see it before."
> "You're enlightened now. Be grateful."

Nick's hard-hat humor never lets him down. Perhaps inevitably, there is a former "garbage guerrilla," now "garbage hustler," with his theories:

> Detwiler said that cities rose on garbage, inch by inch, gaining elevation through the decades as buried debris increased. Garbage always got layered over or pushed to the edges, in a room or in a landscape. But it had its own momentum. It pushed back. It pushed into every space available, dictating construction patterns and altering systems of ritual. And it produced rats and paranoia.

Everywhere, there are abandoned structures and artifacts—"the kind of human junk that deepens the landscape, makes it sadder and lonelier"; along with any number of Pynchon's "preterite"— "wastelings of the lost world, the lost country that exists right here in America." Perhaps unsurprisingly, there is the contention that "waste is the secret history, the underhistory" of our society. And Nick maintains that "what we excrete comes back to consume us." An unattributed, oracular voice (DeLillo's?) announces at one point: "All waste defers to shit. All waste aspires to the condition of shit." Nick's final appearance in the novel is—

of course—at a "waste facility," where he and his granddaughter have brought "the unsorted slop, the gut squalor of our lives" for recycling. The light streaming into the shed gives the machines "a numinous glow," and the moment prompts a final meditation. "Maybe we feel a reverence for waste, for the redemptive qualities of the things we use and discard. Look how they come back to us, alight with a kind of brave aging." Clearly there is waste and waste, since we hardly think of "shit" as coming back to us "with a kind of brave aging."

What there is is waste turned into art—"We took junk and saved it for art," says one artist in the book. "And of course, there are the Watts Towers—a rambling art that has no category"— visited once by Nick, and once by the artist, Klara. "She didn't know a thing so rucked in the vernacular could have such an epic quality."

> She didn't know what this was exactly. It was an amusement park, a temple complex and she didn't know what else. A Delhi bazaar and Italian street feast maybe. A place riddled with epiphanies, that's what it was.

And that is what waste primarily is for DeLillo—epiphanic. That, presumably, is why "waste is a religious thing."

For a Catholic the Epiphany is the manifestation of Christ to the Magi—by extension any manifestation of a god or demigod. Joyce defined an epiphany as "a sudden spiritual manifestation," but without a specifically religious implication. It occurs when a configuration of ordinary things suddenly takes on an extra glow of meaning; when, in Emerson's terms, a "day of facts" suddenly becomes a "day of diamonds," leaving you with, perhaps, a nonarticulable sense of "something understood" (George Herbert). A writer can create secular epiphanic moments—Jack Gladney's exploration of his garbage is an epiphany of a rather dark kind. But simply asserting that something is "riddled with epiphanies" does not, of itself, bring the precious glow. Epiphanies have to be caused rather than insisted on, and *Underworld* suffers somewhat from this failing.

—Tony Tanner, "Afterthoughts on Don DeLillo's *Underworld*."
Raritan: A Quarterly Review 17, no. 4 (Spring 1998): pp. 64–66.

JEREMY GREEN ON TWO KINDS OF VISUAL CULTURE IN THE NOVEL

[Jeremy Green is an Assistant Professor of English at the University of Colorado. In this excerpt, Green argues that the novel presents two kinds of visual culture: one pathological and one nostalgic.]

The episode of the Texas Highway Killer in *Underworld* further plays out in detail the identifications and traumas forged across private and public contexts. A twelve-year-old girl, known by the media as the "Video Kid," accidentally captures one of the murders committed by a serial killer who shoots his victims as they drive along the highway. The footage is then played relentlessly on television, exerting a certain horrified fascination over the viewer. Within the dense texture of echoes, linked motifs, and cross-references that makes up DeLillo's latest novel, the tape of the homicide is connected to a prototype, the Zapruder film, the grainy home movie of the Kennedy assassination shot by a Dallas dressmaker, kept more or less secret for years, and finally seen in public from the mid-seventies on (Klara Sax sees the film during this period, strangely reconfigured as an avant-garde installation). The Zapruder film is, DeLillo has noted, "our major emblem of uncertainty and chaos" ("American" 24), an "atrocity exhibition" (in J. G. Ballard's apt phrase) which appears to show everything but tells nothing. Such uncertainty—and such horror—stem from the problematic interaction of technology and bodies: the crude realities of the film concern the way tissue and bone are affected by high-velocity projectiles; yet the footage is subjected to ever more elaborate scrutiny, as technologies become more discerning with each passing generation. The contrast between the quasi-metaphysical aspirations of technology—the desire to find the ultimate reality, the final truth of the events captured in Zapruder's blurry frames—and the materiality of the body is one of the great themes of the novel and, indeed, of DeLillo's work as a whole. Marvin Lundy, in his passionate three-decade quest for the baseball from the famous 1951 game, resorts to similar technologies, studying the fine-grain of a home movie shot in the Polo Grounds that day, attempting to resolve the extraordinary resonances of a single historical moment, resonances that DeLillo traces across the vast cultural and historical tundra of the Cold War, into a single material fact—a hand grasping a ball.

The tape of the Texas Highway Killer is itself subjected to elaborate technological scrutiny, by Nick Shay's son among others. In this respect, the efforts of technology are invested in the attempt to establish identities once and for all; it is hoped that peering into the grain of the film will allow one finally to determine who fired the shot, who clutched the ball. But at the same time, technology plays an important part in the oscillation between private and public identities, between anonymity and iconicity. DeLillo's exposition of the Highway Killer footage forges a series of links—or, more accurately, traumatic connections established around the relationship of technology and the body—between the intimate, domestic sphere and the exposed, public realm of TV. The video kid is anonymous, merely a chance witness of the events that unfold on the highway; but the camera establishes a complicitous link between her viewing and that of the avid, anonymous watcher of TV, a connection emphasized by the use of the second person: "You know how kids get involved, how the camera shows them that every subject is potentially charged, a million things they never see with the unaided eye. They investigate the meaning of inert objects and dumb pets and they poke at family privacy" (DeLillo, *Underworld* 155). If, at one level, this is a narrative about a "girl [who] got lost and wandered clear-eyed into horror" (157), it is also a story about the (potentially aggressive) desire to see into the privacy of others. Equally, this uncertainty is that of the viewer at home, watching with alarm, but also sadistically trying to get another to watch: "And maybe you're being a little aggressive here, practically forcing your wife to watch" (159).

These complicitous connections, invested as much with the desire to expose privacy to the public gaze as with the horror of such exposure, could not be more different from the ways in which *Underworld* envisages an older kind of collectivity. Across the extended skein of the novel, a contrast may be drawn between the collective established around the spectacle of violence and that founded on unrepeatable proximity in space and time. In the opening scene of the novel, the account of the Dodgers–Giants game, the richly detailed evocation of shared values and experiences is carefully counterposed to the purely abstract identity of an apocalyptic scenario gloomily relished by J. Edgar Hoover. On learning of the second Soviet atomic test, Hoover notes a connection between the individuals in the crowd: "All these people formed by language and climate and popular songs and breakfast foods and the jokes they tell and the cars they drive have never had anything in common so much as this, that they are sitting in the furrow of destruction" (DeLillo, *Underworld* 28). The scene captures a janiform historical perspective: it points back to an older kind of collective identity, based on shared experience and national self-confidence; and it points forward to the pathological public identities founded on shared anxiety and horror. While the structure of the novel retains this dual optic, painstakingly working back into the past from the post–Cold War period, on the one hand, and moving in brief snapshots forward in time in the "Manx Martin" sections, on the other, the geographical and cultural dispersal is gradually reined in as the narrative winds its way back to the Bronx. To this extent, DeLillo's imaginative surveying of a historical break, established most vividly in "The Power of History" as the difference between two kinds of visual culture, one pathological, the other carrying a "moral burnish," tilts towards nostalgia. *Underworld*'s penultimate section, "Arrangement in Gray and Black: Fall 1951–Summer 1952," turns away from the concern with shifting private and public relations and the mechanisms of seriality to root its conception of identity in ethnicity and neighborhood.

—Jeremy Green, "Disaster Footage: Spectacles of Violence in DeLillo's Fiction." *Modern Fiction Studies* 45, no. 3 (Fall 1999): pp. 593–596.

PETER KNIGHT ON THE NOVEL AS HISTORY OF PARANOIA

[Peter Knight teaches American Studies at the University of Nottingham and is the author of *Conspiracy Culture: From the Kennedy Assassination to The X-Files* (2000). In this excerpt, Knight argues that DeLillo's novel provides the materials for a history of paranoia over the last fifty years.]

Elevated to a principle of national policy in the McCarthy years of the Cold War, and then reappropriated as an indispensable attitude of the counterculture in the 1960s, paranoia has become one of the defining characteristics of postwar American politics and culture. In the words of Don DeLillo (once hailed as the "chief shaman of the paranoid school of fiction" [Towers 6]), this is the period in which "paranoia replaced history in American life" (qtd. in O'Toole). As many commentators have pointed out recently, there are very good reasons why conspiratorially infused paranoia should no longer have a hold over the collective imagination, not the least of which is the end of the Cold War and all its attendant anxieties about communist infiltration and mutually assured nuclear destruction. Yet in the last decade it has come to seem that paranoia and conspiracy theories are everywhere: a brief sampling from the last couple of years might include the Oklahoma bombing; the crash of TWA flight 800; the runaway success of *The X-Files*; the self-consciously titled summer 1997 Hollywood blockbuster *Conspiracy Theory*; the inclusion of the very term "conspiracy theory" for the first time in the 1997 supplement to the *OED*; the public declaration by Martin Luther King's family that his death was part of a government conspiracy; and even Hillary Clinton's assertion on national television that "a vast right-wing conspiracy" was against the President. Elaine Showalter's recent book *Hystories* speaks to the common perception there is a "plague of paranoia" spreading through western society. Just when you thought it was safe, the emergence of new fears and fantasies (summed up by President Bush's infamous announcement of a "New World Order") has paradoxically meant a return to the dominance of conspiracy thinking in American life.

A similar conundrum arises in the new world order of American fiction. On the one hand, as Michael Wood suggests, Thomas Pynchon's *Mason and Dixon* and DeLillo's *Underworld* are "post-paranoid" epics: DeLillo's *Libra*, Wood pronounced, was "perhaps the last really good novel of the great age of American paranoia," an age that "faded away somewhere in the early nineties" ("Post-Paranoid" 3). On the other hand, other critics accused *Underworld* of having an unnecessarily paranoid structure, of hinting at connections where none exist; for instance, James Wood, writing in the *New Republic*, declared that *Underworld* "proves, once and for all, the incompatibility of paranoid history with great fiction" ("Black Noise"). So, just when we might expect paranoia to have gone beyond its sell-by date in that six-floor book depository of postwar American literature containing Pynchon, William Burroughs, Norman Mailer, and DeLillo, it seems that *Underworld* has brought the topic out of storage and back onto the shelves.

How can we explain what looks like the simultaneous disappearance and recrudescence of paranoia, in both American literature and society? In this essay I suggest that DeLillo's monumental new novel presents the materials for constructing a secret history of paranoia over the last half-century, which in turn can help explain some of these paradoxes. In brief, *Underworld* revises the anatomy of popular American paranoia that DeLillo has conducted in his previous novels, pushing back the inquiry before the assassination of President John F. Kennedy, which had previously served as the watershed event in his work, and reaching ahead into the as yet unconfigured world beyond the end of the Cold War.

—Peter Knight, "Everything is Connected: *Underworld*'s Secret History of Paranoia." *Modern Fiction Studies* 45, no. 3 (Fall 1999): pp. 811–812.

JESSE KAVADLO ON THE AESTHETICS OF WASTE IN THE NOVEL

[Jesse Kavadlo is an English Instructor at Winona State University. In this excerpt, Kavadlo explores the figurative and the literal implications of waste for both DeLillo and his protagonist.]

Underworld, in its own sprawling way, is a collection of the untold and forgotten stories of the last fifty years, the dregs and waste, an attempt to make something new and artistic, just as Klara's project does. DeLillo presents Nick Shay, an ironic DeLillo double: both grow up in the Bronx, are about the same age, attend Fordham University, and move West away from the Bronx (although, in all fairness, DeLillo moved West only metaphorically, to Westchester). Nick, however, is half Italian, almost a comic distancing device to assure the reader that, despite their similarity, Nick is not Don. In addition, waste management ties into the concept and title of *Underworld*: most obviously, we bury our waste—and our dead—underground; waste is associated with Nick's burdened unconscious; and "underworld" humorously recalls the Mafia and jokes associated with it—in New York, "waste management" was one of the industries most often connected with the mob.

But the novel has more to do with waste than just connotation or Nick's occupation: its seeming excess and sheer length seem an aesthetic reflection of the world described within the novel. In fact, more than being about Nick himself, the novel's explicit subject is waste, literal and figurative: landfills and recycled junk; excrement; nuclear waste; wasted lives, wasted time, the best minds of a generation devoted to waste; burying waste, unearthing waste; civilizations built and ended on account of waste; getting wasted, in terms of both drugs and murder as made emblematic in Nick's murder of George the waiter, the junkie who uses heroin (junk, shit) and gets wasted (killed) for it. *Underworld* shows it all, while self-consciously acknowledging that any excess, even literary, is a kind of waste product: "not nature," as Nathanael West describes art, but "nature digested [...] a sublime excrement" (8) that recycles DeLillo's would-be realism into surrealism. Juxtaposing brand-names, condoms, graffiti, baseball, bombs, and a huge cast of eccentrics, DeLillo's excessive realism recycles, almost parodies, traditional realism into something closer to avant-garde. *Underworld* makes an aesthetic statement about our culture of excess, of trying to make everything bigger and better, all-inclusive, millennial, towering, and imposing, by making an all-consuming, all-connected novel.

If for DeLillo waste is creative fodder for the contemporary novelist, waste, for Nick, becomes the point in and of itself, more than a byproduct or unfortunate result of living. He saw "products as garbage even when they sat gleaming on the store shelves, yet unbought. We didn't say, What kind of casserole will that make? We said, What kind of garbage will that make?"

(121). Garbage is his central preoccupation as well as his official occupation, and all of the products' present usefulness is subsumed by their future as waste. But garbage takes on more meaning than simply the stuff of landfills; waste is all that is left after the last remnants of the Cold War have melted away. Klara is, in that sense, a waste manager, recycling the obsolete warplanes into works of art. As a result, her project is also an attempt to restore a kind of balance. She explains: "Many things that were anchored to the balance of power and the balance of terror seem to be undone, unstuck" (76). The assurances of Us and Them, Good and Evil, and Black and White have all melted into uneasy and uncomfortable shades of gray, with all the products and people left over from a world war that never took place becoming relegated to the status of waste products. If the time preparing for a war that never happened was wasted, then the people left over after the easy balances, the comforting dichotomies and dialectics, are wasted—Nick's unconscious is like a bomb needing to be defused, as dangerous as the nuclear waste at the end of the novel.

—Jesse Kavadlo, "Recycling Authority: Don DeLillo's Waste Management." *Critique: Studies in Contemporary Fiction* 42, no. 4 (Summer 2001): pp. 387–88.

Don DeLillo

"The River Jordan." 1960.

"Take the 'A' Train." 1962.

"Spaghetti and Meatballs." 1965.

"Coming Sun. Mon. Tues." 1966.

"Baghdad Towers West." 1968.

"The Uniforms." 1970.

Americana. 1971.

"In the Men's Room of the Sixteenth Century." 1971.

End Zone. 1972.

"Notes Toward a Definitive Meditation (By Someone Else) on the Novel *Americana.*" 1972.

"Total Loss Weekend." 1972.

Great Jones Street. 1973.

"Notes on 'The Uniforms.'" *Cutting Edges: Young American Fiction for the '70s.* 1973.

Ratner's Star. 1976.

Players. 1977.

Running Dog. 1978.

"Creation." 1979.

The Engineer of Moonlight. 1979.

Amazons (published under pseudonym Cleo Birdwell). 1980.

The Names. 1982.

"American Blood: A Journey Through the Labyrinth of Dallas and JFK." 1983.

"Human Moments in World War III." 1983.

White Noise. 1985.

The Day Room. 1987.

"The Ivory Acrobat." 1988.

Libra. 1988.

"The Runner." 1988.

"Silhouette City: Hitler, Manson, and the Millennium." 1988.

"Rushdie Novel Stirs Passions East and West; Answer to
the Cardinal" (co-written). 1989.

The Rapture of the Athlete Assumed into Heaven (play). 1990.

Mao II. 1991.

"Pafko at the Wall" (later became the prologue to *Underworld*), 1992.

"The Image and the Crowd." 1993.

"The Angel Esmeralda." 1994.

"Salman Rushdie Defense Pamphlet" (co-written with Paul Auster).
1994.

"Notes on 'The Angel Esmeralda.'" *The Best American
Short Stories 1995*. 1995.

"Fitzgerald: the Movie." *F. Scott Fitzgerald at 100:
Centenary Tributes by American Writers*. 1996.

"The Artist Naked in a Cage." 1997.

"The Power of History." 1997.

Underworld. 1997.

"A History of the Writer Alone in a Room." 1999.

Valparaiso. 1999.

"Finding the Dark Heart." *Steppenwolf at 25:
A Photographic Celebration of an Actor's Theater*. 2000.

"The Mystery at the Middle of Ordinary Life." 2000.

The Body Artist. 2001.

"The Fictional Man." *Novel History: Historians and
Novelists Confront America's Past (and Each Other)*. 2001.

"In the Ruins of the Future." 2001.

"Baader-Meinhof." 2002.

Don DeLillo

Alfonso, Ricardo Miguel. *Powerless Fictions? Ethics, Cultural Critique and American Fiction in the Age of Postmodernism.* Amsterdam: Rodopi, 1996.

Birkerts, Sven, ed. *Tolstoy's Dictaphone: Technology and the Muse.* St. Paul, MN: Graywolf, 1996.

Bloom, Harold, ed. *Don DeLillo.* Philadelphia: Chelsea House Publishers, 2002.

———. *White Noise.* Philadelphia: Chelsea House Publishers, 2002.

Branch, Michael, et al., eds. *Reading the Earth: New Directions in the Study of Literature and the Environment.* Moscow, Idaho: University of Idaho Press, 1998.

Brooker, Peter. *New York Fictions: Modernity, Postmodernism, and the New Modern.* London: Longman, 1996.

Carnes, Mark C, ed. *Novel History: Historians and Novelists Confront America's Past (and Each Other).* New York: Simon and Schuster, 2001.

Chenetier, Marc. *Beyond Suspicion: New American Fiction Since 1960.* Trans. Elizabeth A. Houlding. Philadelphia: University of Pennsylvania Press, 1996.

Civello, Paul. *American Literary Naturalism and Its Twentieth-Century Transformations: Frank Norris, Ernest Hemingway, Don DeLillo.* Athens, GA: University of Georgia Press, 1994.

Clarke, Graham ed., *The New American Writing: Essays on American Literature Since 1970.* New York: St. Martin's Press, 1990.

———. "Don DeLillo." *Dictionary of Literary Biography: American Novelists Since WWII.* Vol. 173. 2nd series. Ed. James E. Kibbler, Jr. Detroit: Gale Research, 1996. 14–36.

Dellamora, Richard, ed. *Postmodern Apocalypse: Theory and Cultural Practice at the End.* Philadelphia: University of Pennsylvania, 1995.

Dewey, Joseph. *In a Dark Time: The Apocalyptic Temper in the American Novel of the Nuclear Age.* W. Lafayette, Indiana: Purdue University Press, 1990.

D'haen, Theo, and Hans Bertens, eds. *Narrative Turns and Minor Genres in Postmodernism.* Amsterdam: Rodopi, 1995.

Engler, Bernd, and Kurt Muller, eds. *Historiographic Metafiction in Modern American and Canadian Literature.* Paderborn, Germany: Ferdinand Schoningh, 1994.

Frow, John. *Time and Commodity Culture.* Oxford: Clarendon Press, 1997.

Giordano, Paolo A., and Anthony Julian Tamburri, eds. *Beyond the Margin: Readings in Italian Americana.* Cranbury, NY: Farleigh Dickinson UP, 1998.

Glotfelty, Cheryll, and Harold Fromm, eds. *The Ecocriticism Reader: Landmarks in Literary Ecology.* Athens, Georgia: The University of Georgia Press, 1996.

Hantke, Steffen. *Conspiracy and Paranoia in Contemporary American Fiction: The Works of Don DeLillo and Joseph McElroy.* Frankfurt: Peter Lang, 1994.

Johnson, Diane. *Terrorists and Novelists.* New York: Knopf, 1982.

Keesey, Douglas. *Don DeLillo.* Twayne's United States Authors Series. New York: Twayne, 1993.

Kerridge, Richard, and Neil Sammells, eds. *Writing the Environment: Ecocriticism and Literature.* London: Zed, 1998.

Kraus, Elisabeth, and Carolin Auer, eds. *Simulacrum America: The USA and the Popular Media.* Rochester, NY; Camden House, 2000.

LeClair, Thomas, and Larry McCaffery. *Anything Can Happen: Interviews with Contemporary American Novelists.* Urbana: University of Illinois Press, 1983.

LeClair, Thomas. *In the Loop: Don DeLillo and the Systems Novel.* Chicago: University of Illinois Press, 1987.

Lentricchia, Frank, ed. *Introducing Don DeLillo.* Durham, N.C.: Duke University Press, 1991.

————, ed. *New Essays on* White Noise. Cambridge: Cambridge University Press, 1991.

McCaffery, Larry, ed. *Postmodern Fiction: A Bio-Bibliographical Guide.* New York: Greenwood Press, 1986.

Mengham, Rod, ed. *An Introduction to Contemporary Fiction: International Writing in English Since 1970.* Cambridge, England: Polity, 1999.

Moran, Joe. *Star Authors: Literary Celebrity in America.* London: Pluto Press, 2000.

Nadeau, Robert. *Readings from the New Book on Nature: Physics and Metaphysics in the Modern Novel.* Amherst: University of Massachusetts Press, 1981.

Osteen, Mark. *American Magic and Dread: Don DeLillo's Dialogue with Culture.* Philadelphia: University of Pennsylvania, 2000.

————, ed. *White Noise: Text and Criticism.* New York: Penguin Books, 1998.

Penrod, Diane, ed. *Miss Grundy Doesn't Teach Here Any More: Popular Culture and the Composition Classroom.* Portsmouth, NH: Boynton/Cook, 1997.

Reid, Ian. *Narrative Exchanges.* New York: Routledge, 1992.

Ruppersburg, Hugh, and Tim Engles, eds. *Critical Essays on Don DeLillo.* New York: G.K. Hall, 2000.

Saltzman, Arthur M. *Designs of Darkness in Contemporary American Fiction.* Philadelphia: University of Pennsylvania Press, 1990.

Simmons, Philip E. *Deep Surfaces: Mass Culture & History in Postmodern American Fiction.* Athens: University of Georgia Press, 1997.

Tabbi, Joseph. *Postmodern Sublime: Technology and American Writing from Mailer to Cyberpunk.* New York: Cornell University Press, 1995.

Umphlett, Wiley Lee, ed. *American Sport Culture: The Humanistic Dimensions.* Lewisburg: Bucknell UP, 1985.

Weinstein, Arnold. *Nobody's Home: Speech, Self and Place in American Fiction from Hawthorne to DeLillo.* New York: Oxford University Press, 1993.

White, Patti. *Gatsby's Party: The System and the List in Contemporary Narrative*. West Lafayette, Indiana: Purdue University Press, 1992.

Wright, Will, and Steve Kaplan, eds. *The Image of Technology in Literature, the Media, and Society*. Pueblo, CO: Society for the Interdisciplinary Study of Social Imagery, University of Southern Colorado, 1994.

ACKNOWLEDGMENTS

"The Fiction of Don DeLillo" by David Bosworth. From *Boston Review* 8, no. 2 (April 1983): p. 30. © 1983 by the Boston Critic, Inc. Reprinted by permission.

"Discussing the Untellable: Don DeLillo's *The Names*" by Paula Bryant. From *Critique: Studies in Modern Fiction* 29, no. 1 (Fall 1987): pp. 17–19. Reprinted with permission of the Helen Dwight Reid Educational Foundation. Published by Heldref Publications, 1319 Eighteenth St., NW, Washington, DC 20036-1802. Copyright © 1987.

"Murdering Words: Language in Action in Don DeLillo's *The Names*" by Matthew J. Morris. From *Contemporary Literature* 30, no. 1 (Spring 1989): pp. 115–117. © 1989 by *Contemporary Literature*. Reprinted by permission.

"Alphabetic Pleasures: *The Names*" by Dennis A. Foster. From *The South Atlantic Quarterly* 89, no. 2 (Spring 1990): pp. 395–397. © 1990 by *The South Atlantic Quarterly*. Reprinted by permission.

"Postmodern Romance: Don DeLillo and the Age of Conspiracy" by John A. McClure. From *Introducing Don DeLillo*, ed. Frank Lentricchia, (Durham, NC: Duke University Press, 1991): pp. 111–113. © 1991 by Duke University Press. Reprinted by permission.

"Lee Harvey Oswald and the Modern Subject: History and Intertextuality in Don DeLillo's *Libra*, *The Names*, and *Mao II* " by Thomas Carmichael. From *Contemporary Literature* 34, no. 2 (Summer 1993): pp. 212–214. © 1993 by *Contemporary Literature*. Reprinted by permission.

" 'Das Schaudern ist der Meschheit bestes Teil': The Sublime as Part of the Mythic Strategy in Don DeLillo's *The Names*" by Maria Moss. From *Amerikastudien: American Studies* 43, no. 3 (1998): pp. 489–490. © 1998 by Maria Moss. Reprinted by permission.

"Last Days: Millenial Hysteria in Don DeLillo's *Mao II*" by Jeremy Green. From *Essays and Studies* (1995): pp. 131–133. © 1995 by *Essays and Studies*. Reprinted by permission.

"Can the Intellectual Still Speak? The Example of Don DeLillo's *Mao II*" by Sylvia Caporale Bizzini. From *Critical Quarterly* 37, no. 2 (Summer 1995): pp. 108-109. © 1995 by *Critical Quarterly*. Reprinted by permission.

"Don DeLillo: *Americana, Mao II*, and *Underworld*" by Adam Begley. From *Southwest Review* 82, no. 4 (1997): pp. 489–491. © 1997 by *Southwest Review*. Reprinted by permission.

Simmons, Ryan. "What is a Terrorist? Contemporary Authorship, the Unabomber, and DeLillo's *Mao II*." *Modern Fiction Studies* 45, no. 3 (Fall 1999): pp. 687–689. © 1999 by Johns Hopkins University Press. Reprinted by permission of Johns Hopkins University Press.

"Becoming Incorporated: Spectacular Authorship and DeLillo's *Mao II*" by Mark Osteen. From *Modern Fiction Studies* 45, no. 3 (Fall 1999): pp. 655–657. © 1999 by *Modern Fiction Studies*. Reprinted by permission.

"Don DeLillo and the Myth of the Author-Recluse" by Joe Moran. From *Journal of American Studies* 34, no. 1 (April 2000): pp. 145–147. © 2000 by *Journal of American Studies*. Reprinted by permission.

"Wallpaper Mao: Don DeLillo, Andy Warhol, and Seriality" by Jeffrey Karnicky. From *Critique: Studies in Contemporary Fiction* 42, no. 4 (Summer 2001): pp. 339, 340-341. Reprinted with permission of the Helen Dwight Reid Educational Foundation. Published by Heldref Publications, 1319 Eighteenth St., NW, Washington, DC 20036-1802. Copyright © 2001.

"Libra as Postmodern Critique" by Frank Lentricchia. From *The South Atlantic Quarterly* 89, no. 2 (Spring 1990): pp. 438–441. © 1990 by *The South Atlantic Quarterly*. Reprinted by permission.

"Undoing the Naturalistic Novel: Don Delillo's *Libra*" by Paul Civello. From *Arizona Quarterly* 48, no. 2 (Summer 1992): pp. 35–38. © 1992 by *Arizona Quarterly*. Reprinted by permission.

"Loose Ends and Patterns of Coincidence in Don DeLillo's *Libra*" by Heinz Ickstadt. From *Historiographic Metafiction in Modern American and Canadian Literature*, ed. Bernd Engler and Kurt Muller, (Paderborn, Germany: Ferdinand Schoningh, 1994): pp. 305–308. © 1994 by Heinz Ickstadt. Reprinted by permission.

"Superlinear Fiction or Historical Diagram: Don DeLillo's *Libra*" by John Johnston. From *Modern Fiction Studies* 40, no. 2 (Summer 1994): pp. 330–332. © 1994 by *Modern Fiction Studies*. Reprinted by permission.

"History, Biography, and Narrative in Don DeLillo's *Libra*" by Glen Thomas. From *Twentieth Century Literature* 43, no. 1 (Spring 1997): pp. 107–109. © 1997 by *Twentieth Century Literature*. Reprinted by permission.

"Traversing the Fantasies of the JFK Assassination: Conspiracy and Contingency in Don DeLillo's *Libra*" by Skip Willman. From *Contemporary Literature* 39, no. 3 (Fall 1998): pp. 421–422. © 1998 by *Contemporary Literature*. Reprinted by permission.

"Why Oswald Missed: Don DeLillo's *Libra*" by David T. Courtwright. From *Novel History: Historians and Novelists Confront America's Past (and Each Other)*, ed. Mark C. Carnes, (New York: Simon and Schuster, 2001): pp. 86–87, 87–88, 89. © 2001 by Simon and Schuster. Reprinted by permission.

"DeLillo's *Libra* and the Real" by Stuart Hutchinson. From *The Cambridge Quarterly* 30, no. 2 (2001): pp. 122–124. © 2001 by *The Cambridge Quarterly*. Reprinted by permission.

"'Thinking it Through Completely': The Interpretation of Nuclear Culture" by Michael W. Messmer. From *The Centennial Review* 32, no. 4 (Fall 1988): pp. 402–404. © 1988 by *The Centennial Review*. Reprinted by permission.

"The Last Things Before the Last: Notes on *White Noise*" by John Frow. From *The South Atlantic Quarterly* 89, no. 2 (Spring 1990): pp. 415–417. © 1990 by *The South Atlantic Quarterly*. Reprinted by permission.

"Postmodernism and DeLillo's *White Noise*" by N. H. Reeve and Richard Kerridge. From *The Cambridge Quarterly* 23, no. 4 (1994): pp. 318–320. © 1994 by *The Cambridge Quarterly*. Reprinted by permission.

"The Postnatural Novel: Toxic Consciousness in Fiction of the 1980s" by Cynthia Deitering. From *The Ecocriticism Reader: Landmarks in Literary Ecology*, ed. Cheryll Glotfelty and Harold Fromm, (Athens, Georgia: The University of Georgia Press, 1996): pp. 196–197, 198. © 1996 by Cynthia Deitering. Reprinted by permission.

"Globalization in America: The Case of Don DeLillo's *White Noise*" by Thomas Peyser. From *CLIO: A Journal of Literature, History and the Philosophy of History* 25, no. 3 (Spring 1996): pp. 255–257. © 1996 by *CLIO*. Reprinted by permission.

"Don DeLillo's Postmodern Pastoral" by Dana Phillips. From *Reading the Earth: New Directions in the Study of Literature and the Environment*, ed. Michael P. Branch et al., (Moscow, Idaho: University of Idaho Press, 1998): pp. 236–238. © 1998 by University of Idaho Press. Reprinted by permission.

Engles, Tim. "'Who Are You, Literally?': Fantasies of the White Self in *White Noise*." *Modern Fiction Studies* 45, no. 3 (Fall 1999): pp. 761–763. © 1999 by *Modern Fiction Studies*. Reprinted by permission of John Hopkins University Press.

"Deft Acceleration: The Occult Geometry of Time in *White Noise*" by Marion Muirhead. From *Critique: Studies in Contemporary Fiction* 42, no. 4 (Summer 2001): pp. 404–405. Reprinted with permission of the Helen Dwight Reid Educational Foundation. Published by Heldref Publications, 1319 Eighteenth St., NW, Washington, DC 20036-1802. Copyright © 2001.

"Exile on Main Street" by David Remnick. From *The New Yorker* 15 September 1997: p. 44. © 1997 by David Remnick. Reprinted by permission. All rights reserved.

"Blasts From the Past" by James Wolcott. From *The New Criterion* 16, no. 4 (December 1997): 66–68. © 1997 by *The New Criterion*. Reprinted by permission.

"Afterthoughts on Don DeLillo's *Underworld*" by Tony Tanner. Reprinted by permission from *Raritan: A Quarterly Review*, Vol. 17 No. 4 (Spring 1998). © 1998 by *Raritan*.

Green, Jeremy. "Disaster Footage: Spectacles of Violence in DeLillo's Fiction" *Modern Fiction Studies* 45, no. 3 (Fall 1999): pp. 593–596. © 1999 by *Modern Fiction Studies*. Reprinted by permission of Johns Hopkins University Press.

Knight, Peter. "Everything is Connected: *Underworld*'s Secret History of Paranoia" From *Modern Fiction Studies* 45, no. 3 (Fall 1999): pp. 811–812. © 1999 by *Modern Fiction Studies*. Reprinted by permission of Johns Hopkins University Press.

of, 64, 91, 129–144; Sister Edgar in, 126, 128, 130; Esmerelda in, 128, 130; Brian Glassic in, 125–126, 129, 136; Gracie in, 128, 130; J. Edgar Hoover in, 125, 127, 129, 131, 134, 140; Marvin Lundy in, 126–127, 130, 138; George Manza in, 126–130; Cotter Martin in, 125–126, 129–131; Manx Martin in, 125–127, 130, 140; Ismael Munoz in, 126, 128, 130; paranoia in, 140–142; plot summary of, 125–128; portrayal of Lenny Bruce in, 133–135; Klara Sax in, 125–129, 137–138, 142, 144; Marian Shay in, 126–127, 129; Matt Shay in, 126, 130; Nick Shay in, 125–130, 132, 136–137, 139, 142–143; Rosemary Shay in, 126; visual culture in, 138–140; Chuckie Wainwright in, 127–130; Charles Wainwright in, 127, 130; waste-inspired epiphanies in, 135–137

VALPARAISO, 15

WHITE NOISE, 96–124, antithesis of Jack's paranoia in, 108–110; Babette in, 96–98, 100–101, 103, 108; blocked pastoral impulse in, 116–119; Dana Breedlove in, 96–98, 101; Malcolm Browner in, 102; Tweedy Browner in, 96–97, 102; characters in, 100–102; construction of typicality in, 105–107; critical views on, 14, 58, 64, 91, 103–124; Vernon Dickey in, 98–99, 101; Bee Gladney in, 96–97, 102; Heinrich Gladney in, 96–98, 100, 102–103, 106, 121; Jack Gladney in, 96–103, 106, 108, 110, 112, 117–123, 137; Steffie Gladney in, 96–98, 101, 103; globalization in, 113–116; "hyperreality" in, 103–105; Willie Mink/ Mr. Gray in, 99–101; novel's plot structure in, 122–124; Bob Pardee in, 96–97, 100, 102; Denise Pardee in, 96–98, 100, 118; plot summary of, 96–99; racialized perception in, 119–122; Winnie Richards in, 98–99, 101; Murray Jay Siskind in, 96–100, 107, 109, 118–119; Janet Savory in, 96, 100, 102; toxic consciousness in, 110–113; Mr. Treadwell in, 97, 101; Wilder in, 96, 101, 107–109